NORTH CAROLINA'S
SHINING HOUR

IMAGES AND VOICES FROM WORLD WAR II

ON THE COVER (FROM BACK TO FRONT):
Top Row: USS *North Carolina*, Arthur and Falls Price, Frances Simpson Best, William C. Lee,
Jack Lucas receiving the Medal of Honor, Maj. Thomas Ferebee, parade at Camp Davis.

Middle Row: Petie Lynn Bass and her mother Ruth Lynn, William H. Wood, a boy breaks the bank to buy
bonds, Dorothy and Norris Dearmon, scrap metal drive in Raleigh, John Bumgarner, H.G. Jones.

Bottom Row: Blanchard Watts, Bud Hampton and his unit on Saipan, Camp Lejeune War Dog
Detachment, Raymond Wagoner, Doc Long and his friends in Europe, the Cloudbusters, Eddie Hart,
WASP pilots Viola Thompson and Mary Clifford, J.R. Holden and Minka.

NORTH CAROLINA'S SHINING HOUR

IMAGES AND VOICES FROM WORLD WAR II

EDITED BY MARY BEST

DESIGNED BY LARRY WILLIAMS

CONTRIBUTORS:
DAVID LA VERE, DIANE SILCOX-JARRETT, AND JIMMY TOMLIN

PUBLISHED BY

Our State
NORTH CAROLINA
BOOKS

ISBN 0-9723396-5-5

Published by:
Our State Books
P.O. Box 4552
Greensboro, N.C. 27404
800.948.1409
ourstate.com

Printed in Winston-Salem, North Carolina, by Jostens Inc.

Publisher: **BERNARD MANN**
Executive Vice President: **LYNN TUTTEROW**
Editor and Associate Publisher: **MARY BEST**
Art Director and Designer: **LARRY WILLIAMS**
Copy Editors: **AMANDA HIATT** and **BETTY WORK**
Marketing Director: **AMY JO WOOD**
Marketing Assistant: **DEBBIE WEST**
Production Director: **CHERYL BISSETT**
Distribution Manager: **ERICA DERR**

Library of Congress Cataloging-in-Publication Data

La Vere, David.
 North Carolina's Shining Hour : Images and Voices from World War II /
by David La Vere, Diane Silcox-Jarrett, and Jimmy Tomlin ; edited by Mary Best; designed
by Larry Williams.
     p. cm.
 Includes bibliographical references and index.
 ISBN 0-9723396-5-5 (pbk. : alk. paper)
 1. World War, 1939-1945--North Carolina. 2. North Carolina--History--20th
century. 3. World War, 1939-1945--Personal narratives, American. I.
Silcox-Jarrett, Diane. II. Tomlin, Jimmy, 1962- III. Best, Mary, 1962- IV.
Title.
 D769.85.N8L3 2005
 940.54'81756--dc22
                              2004030586

LEST WE FORGET ...

RIGHT ON THE NOSE James R. Starns of Wilmington *(third from the left)* stands with the crew of his P-51 Mustang — appropriately named the *Tar Heel*.

CONTENTS

8 INTRODUCTION
by Mary Best

CHAPTER ONE
14 SHOCK
DECEMBER 7, 1941

CHAPTER TWO
30 DEFENSE
NORTH CAROLINA'S MILITARY MACHINE

CHAPTER THREE
60 COURAGE
COMBATING AN AXIS OF ENEMIES

CHAPTER FOUR
118 HOME FRONT
NORTH CAROLINA DURING WARTIME

CHAPTER FIVE
146 VICTORY
A NEW ROAD HOME

CHAPTER SIX
162 REMEMBRANCE
NORTH CAROLINA'S "FINEST HOUR"

176 ACKNOWLEDGMENTS
176 CONTRIBUTORS
177 BIBLIOGRAPHY
178 INDEX
179 ABOUT OUR STATE BOOKS

SCRAPBOOKS

"To some generations, much is given. Of other generations, much is expected,"
Franklin Roosevelt said. "This generation of Americans has a rendezvous with destiny."

On a wintry afternoon some 30 years ago, I came across two dusty scrapbooks in a closet in the house where I was raised. My parents had tucked them away with various other remnants of their lives before marriage and children — Army uniforms, finely tailored dresses, North Carolina souvenirs, boxes of fancy hats. Knowing in my young heart that it was wrong to violate the privacy of these sweet souls, I sneaked off to my room with the scrapbooks to learn what secrets they held.

One slim album, about the size of a magazine, chronicled two chapters in my father's life. Dozens of fading photographs glued onto water-stained pages showed him as a boy growing up in the soundside community of Stumpy Point in the 1920s — a two-year-old with curly blond hair holding a kitten; a picture taken on his first day of school. A second set of pictures showed him as a grown man — graduation day at East Carolina Teachers College; his first job as a teacher. On the inside back cover, a newspaper photo of my mom.

The second scrapbook — mustier, much thicker — told the chapter of my father's life missing from the first book: his life as a soldier. At first the images were of him and his Army buddies, full of laughter. There were several pictures of a woman I assumed was his girlfriend at one time. One page held a dozen or so coins from different countries, including one with a Swastika. But most of the pictures showed bombed-out homes, destroyed towns, men cooking from the back of a huge truck, a weathered old woman draped in a shawl and scurrying down the street with firewood on her back. Faces darkened by war, the hungry, the homeless, the hurt.

I knew why the scrapbooks had remained hidden away. I returned them to their proper place and never mentioned what I had seen.

Nearly every North Carolina family has stories of World War II, stories of bravery, of sacrifice, of hard work. My family's story starts with my father, Will Best. He graduated from high school in 1940 and was working at the Norfolk Naval Yard as a welder when he joined the Army in 1943. He marched from France to Berlin in 1944-1945; he was there during one of Europe's coldest winters on record. On the home front, Frances Simpson put off plans to earn a degree in music in order to take a job in a

CONTINUED ON PAGE 11

army ___ ___

Malefield Germany

au __ Lane Junior

Spangenburg May 1945

CONTINUED FROM PAGE 8

defense plant and enroll in a nurses' training program. She entertained the nursing cadets and sisters at St. Leo's Hospital in Greensboro by playing the piano at daily chapel services. Despite the grim reality of the war years, my mother enjoyed those youthful days. At night, she and her friends sneaked across the street to dance with G.I.s at the Overseas Replacement Depot, lindy-hopping and jitterbugging to the Big Band sounds of the Andrews Sisters and Glenn Miller.

After the war, my father used the G.I. Bill to become a teacher. My mother finished college and became a music teacher. They met in my mother's hometown of Stokesdale, dated, and, in 1951, wed. The hard times of the war dimmed for my parents as years went by, and the good memories lingered. On New Year's Eve, they would waltz to the 1940s song "As Time Goes By." My mom would play favorite "Hit Parade" tunes on the piano. My dad regaled us with stories of his lighter moments as a soldier — seeing the white cliffs of Dover, meeting up with his buddies in Paris, playing pranks on Soviet troops in postwar Berlin, and sending "coded" letters to my grandmother.

For as long as I can remember, a photograph of President Roosevelt hung on the wall over my grandmother's kitchen range, a reminder of the almost holy reverence she held for him. In her eyes, he not only rescued the nation from the Depression and defended democracy, but also brought her youngest son safely home.

My father had bought her that kitchen stove with money he saved from his Army wages; it was the first electric range she had ever had. There's a picture in his World War II scrapbook that documents this milestone. The white enamel Kenmore, FDR, and my father hugging his mother.

In essence, *North Carolina's Shining Hour: Images and Voices from World War II* is also a scrapbook, filled with North Carolina memories and impressions, legends and legacies. It is also a book about people like my mother and father, everyday North Carolinians who gave and sacrificed because it was the right thing to do. The stories and images on the following pages are intended to acknowledge, at least in a small way, our appreciation for their indomitable spirit. Time will not forget their names or their deeds; neither should we.

Mary

Mary Best
Editor

STARS AND STRIPES FOREVER Flags fly high as soldiers at Camp Davis march across the parade ground in 1943.

CHAPTER ONE

SHOCK

DECEMBER 7, 1941

"We may acknowledge that our enemies have performed a brilliant feat of deception, perfectly timed and executed with great skill. It was a thoroughly dishonorable deed, but we must face the fact that modern warfare as conducted in the Nazi manner is a dirty business. We don't like it — we didn't want to get in it — but we are in it and we're going to fight it with everything we've got. ... We are going to win the war, and we are going to win the peace that follows."

— *Franklin D. Roosevelt, December 9, 1941*

SURPRISE ATTACK More than 450 Japanese planes rip through the U.S. naval base at Pearl Harbor on the island of Oahu, destroying 21 ships in the U.S. Pacific Fleet. One of the day's most horrifying explosions comes when the USS *Shaw* is bombed in dry dock. Lasting less than two hours, the carefully planned raid leaves 2,403 Americans dead and 1,178 wounded.

PARADISE LOST

The Bombing of Pearl Harbor

War came to America on a quiet Sunday morning half a world away from North Carolina. Few days in history are remembered as vividly. All Americans who were old enough on December 7, 1941, to remember that day know the exact moment they heard. Telegraph, telephone, and teletype relayed the news from Hawaii to the mainland. Everywhere on the radio was heard: "We interrupt this program to bring you a special news bulletin. The Japanese have attacked Pearl Harbor, Hawaii, by air."

The reaction was electric: anger and sorrow first, followed by a great surge of patriotism. "We have awakened a sleeping giant and instilled in him a terrible resolve," Japanese Admiral Yamamoto would later reflect. In North Carolina and across the land, citizens put aside personal wants and needs and pulled together to fight the "good war." And in so doing, forever changed history.

DRAFT No. 1   December 7, 1941.

PROPOSED MESSAGE TO THE CONGRESS

Yesterday, December 7, 1941, a date which will live in ~~world history~~ *infamy* — *Japan*

the United States of America was ~~simultaneously~~ *suddenly* and deliberately attacked

by naval and air forces of the Empire of Japan, ~~without warning~~ .

The United States was at the moment at peace with that nation and was

~~continuing the~~ *still in* conversation*s* with its Government and its Emperor looking

toward the maintenance of peace in the Pacific. Indeed, one hour after,

Japanese air squadrons had commenced bombing in *Oahu* ~~Hawaii and the Philippines~~

the Japanese Ambassador to the United States and his colleague delivered

to the Secretary of State a formal reply to a ~~former~~ *recent American* message, ~~from the~~

~~Secretary~~ . *While* This reply ~~contained a statement~~ *stated* that diplomatic negotiations *it seemed useless to continue the existing diplomatic negotiations*

~~must be considered at an end, but~~ *it* contained no threat ~~and no~~ *or* hint *of an* *war or*

armed attack.

It will be recorded that the distance ~~of Manila, and especially~~ of

Hawaii, from Japan make*s* it obvious that the*y* attack ~~were~~ *was* deliberately

planned many days *or even weeks* ago. During the intervening time the Japanese Govern-

ment has deliberately sought to deceive the United States by false

statements and expressions of hope for continued peace.

SURVIVOR
JAMES LANCASTER

On the evening of December 6, 1941, Seaman 1C James Lancaster and his buddies aboard the USS *Arizona* were drinking and arguing about the chances of the Japanese bombing their ship. The young sailor from Selma argued, "we were sitting ducks out there." An orderly came around to tell them to quiet down, and that was the end of that.

Up early the next morning, Lancaster heard the roar of planes. "I had never seen so many planes coming overhead. When I saw those rising suns under the wings, I knew what was coming." As he dashed to his battle station, a bomb exploded amidships. He came to in the water, gasping for breath. "The water was on fire. The *Arizona* was one huge fireball.

"Men were screaming all around me — a sound I will never forget. At first it was every man for himself. You just reacted, you were in such shock. I did the first thing that popped into my mind."

Diving under the burning water, he finally reached the captain's boat and started reaching for men around him. Although seriously injured himself, "I kept pulling them in, thinking if I got them ashore then they would live." The *Arizona* sank with more than 1,100 crew. Lancaster would never again see his friends from the night before.

After carrying 10 men to Ford Island, Lancaster made a second trip and rescued six or seven more men from the bay. "I wanted to go out again, but they wouldn't let me. I was out of my mind by then and not thinking straight."

Lancaster was taken to the air-raid shelter and cleaned up. "I had oil all over me and my hair was gone. A lady handed me a pair of pants and a necktie. I put on the pants and tied them with the tie. That was the extent of my clothes for several days."

The North Carolinian was one of 289 men on the *Arizona* to survive, but was reported missing in action by the Navy because he spent six days as a volunteer aboard the battleship *West Virginia*. "My parents had no idea what had happened to me until I came home. Since they hadn't gotten any information, my mother thought I was dead. But my dad kept saying he had the feeling I was alive."

Several months later, Lancaster stepped off a bus in his hometown. A crowd gathered, and neighbors raced to tell his folks the good news. "It's a small town and some of the people knew my parents were at the grocery store and went to get them. My mother let out a cry like you never heard before. I was so glad to be home."

— *Diane Silcox-Jarrett*

THE SOUND AND FURY A Japanese bomb slams into the *Arizona*, igniting a million pounds of gunpowder and sending the battleship to the bottom of the bay in nine minutes. It is the greatest single loss of the day, killing 1,177 sailors and Marines, among them at least six North Carolinians.

THE LONG WAIT In North Carolina, James Lancaster's mom and dad will not learn for months that he survived the sinking of the *Arizona*.

TO THE RESCUE

When Rutherford County native Edgar Green *(above left with brother Dwight)* answered the phone at Pearl Harbor's 14th Naval District Headquarters, Green figured the person on the other end was drunk when he heard the caller yelling, "The Japanese are attacking!" When he rushed outside a minute later, Green saw the horrifying truth. "I could see the teeth of the Japanese pilot," he said, according to *Rutherford County in World War II* by Anita Price Davis and James M. Walker. "I immediately drew my .45 and began shooting at the Japanese plane." Green then focused his attention on life-saving efforts. "We set up the first-aid station on the pier at Ford Island where we would take the people we picked out of the water. I worked from Sunday 7 a.m. until Wednesday at 4 a.m. rescuing survivors and helping the injured and dying. I ate one bologna sandwich during the entire 69-hour period."

WATERY INFERNO The *West Virginia* burns for more than 24 hours after being repeatedly hit by torpedoes and bombs.

Pearl Harbor, August 1941

FROM HERE TO ETERNITY Named by native Hawaiians for the pearl oysters that were once in abundance, Pearl Harbor was more than a vacation wonderland on the eve of World War II. Following a massive military buildup, by 1940 the ancient estuary was home to the U.S. Pacific Fleet. "Battleship Row" — where five U.S. battleships sank on December 7 — was believed to be one of the world's most impregnable military outposts.

CORBIS

A MONTH OF SUNDAYS

"... the wreckage at Pearl was appalling.
... Reconstruction is under way, but
the hundreds of men struggling to raise
sunken ships and repair shattered ones,
to clean up the piles of debris and bring
order out of the apparently hopeless
confusion, were like ants tunneling at
a mountain."

— *A North Carolina pilot quoted in* North
Carolina's Role in World War II
by Sarah McCulloh Lemmon

INNOCENCE LOST

A Sunday in North Carolina

North Carolinians woke to a fair but cold Sunday. In High

Point, residents opened the *Enterprise* to read about the city's annual Empty Stocking

Fund. In Charlotte, Dixie Football League fans were looking forward to the afternoon's

matchup between the Charlotte Clippers and the Norfolk Shamrocks at Memorial

Stadium. In Wilmington, the thousands of onlookers who had watched the USS

Zebulon B. Vance coast into the Cape Fear River were still marveling at the previous

day's launch. Tar Heel churches filled as worshipers gathered to celebrate the

second Sunday of Advent. And while the state was enjoying an economic boom from

burgeoning military installations and manufacturing, most North Carolinians did not

feel the imminence of war. By early afternoon, however, the news from Pearl Harbor

was all anyone was talking about. Thoughts of Christmas cheer turned to fear.

OFF SHE GOES The North Carolina Shipbuilding Co. launches its first Liberty ship – the *Zebulon B. Vance* – in Wilmington on December 6. Originally, the Maritime Commission announced the ship would be the *Francis Marion*, named for South Carolina's Revolutionary War hero known as the "Swamp Fox," but North Carolinians protested; as a result, the ship was christened in memory of the Old North State's Civil War governor.

SIGN ME UP

Among all the manifestations of spirit brought suddenly into existence by the events of Sunday and Monday is the following communication received by Board No. 1 of the Selective Service System in Salisbury:

"Gentlemen, last June I filled in my questionnaire as a conscientious objector. I was sincerely opposed to participation in a foreign war at the time — and I probably had a lot of company. The events of the last two days have caused me to change my mind completely. Conscientious objector, hell! I'm ready to go ... I would like to request that you permit me to change the questionnaire or allow me the privilege of filling out another. If that cannot be done, please attach this statement to the old one."

The Salisbury board is complying.

— The State: A Weekly Survey of North Carolina,
December 13, 1941

HERE'S JOHNNY

For four years Pvt. John W. Scism has been listed on Army rolls as AWOL, but this week he gave himself up to military police at Fort Bragg and said that he wanted to serve his country now that it is at war. His uniform was restored and he was assigned to duty without any punishment for his long "vacation." ... Since the outbreak of the war with Japan, MP headquarters at Fort Bragg have reported that four other men listed as absent without leave have returned to military service.

— The State: A Weekly Survey of North Carolina,
December 20, 1941

...we here highly resolve that these dead shall not have died in vain...

REMEMBER DEC. 7th!

REMEMBER PEARL HARBOR

Winston Churchill's words "sweat and blood and tears" summarize better than anything else that which the American people may expect during the year 1942. ... The time when only men at the front carried the burden of war has passed. Today war is everybody's business, victory is the key to everyone's future, and defeat would mean only one thing, slavery. Remember Pearl Harbor!

— The State: A Weekly Survey of North Carolina,
December 27, 1941

CALL TO ARMS The Office of War Information swiftly issues the poster above, emblazoned with the words from Lincoln's Gettysburg Address, in early 1942.

NEXT STOP, FORT BRAGG Following the invasion of Pearl Harbor, new recruits flood the Fayetteville Army base. Between 1940 and 1942, it grows from 5,400 to more than 100,000 soldiers.

FROM THIS DAY FORWARD
NANCY KIMMONS

When Nancy Kimmons heard the news about Pearl Harbor, it meant one thing — the deferment of a dream. In only three weeks, her betrothed, John, would have completed his National Guard obligation at Fort Jackson, South Carolina. He was going to return to Statesville, where the young couple had met and become sweethearts. He would establish a career, find a home for them, and they would get married. Kimmons was a student at Woman's College in Greensboro at the time. "We had our life all planned."

They planned a large church wedding in Statesville for late June — a few weeks after Nancy's graduation. After the invitations were mailed, however, John was transferred to a base in Louisiana. He asked his warrant officer for permission to go home for the wedding, but was denied. Then he asked permission to petition the colonel for a furlough.

"I can't imagine you making any kind of wedding plans in wartime," the colonel replied. "I can't give you a furlough. I can't even give myself a furlough."

"We had our life all planned."

But with Pearl Harbor, they knew those plans would change. The United States certainly would declare war, and John would not be discharged from the Guard. "I wasn't even thinking about the war and the magnitude of it. I was upset because I knew it was going to change things in my life."

Sure enough, John ended up spending five years in the military. He and Nancy were able to get married, however, thanks to a crusty colonel who had a soft spot in his heart.

John just smiled. "I know you can't give yourself a furlough," he said, "but you could give me one if you wanted to. I've got a cute little girl waiting for me."

The colonel relented, and the couple tied the knot in Statesville on June 27, 1942 — and they immediately returned to Louisiana.

— *Jimmy Tomlin*

POSING FOR THE FUTURE Nancy and John Kimmons smile in anticipation of their long-awaited nuptials in 1942.

CHAPTER TWO

DEFENSE

NORTH CAROLINA'S MILITARY MACHINE

"If it was a den of rattlesnakes opposing Hitler, I would aid and abet them."
— *U.S. Senator Josiah W. Bailey of North Carolina, quoted in*
The State: A Weekly Survey of North Carolina, *September 6, 1941*

AND ONE AND TWO From March 1943 to April 1944, Greensboro's Basic Training Center #10 initiates trainloads of new recruits into the U.S. Army Air Forces. In 1944, the facility becomes the Overseas Replacement Depot for the eastern United States.

Join Up!

One hundred men and boys spilled into the Army recruiting office at Charlotte bright and early on Monday, December 8, and for many days following.

Some in line were veterans of World War I. Others were barely in high school. The Navy office at Raleigh took in a record 78 enlistees in one day. Overwhelmed recruiting offices extended business hours and brought in extra staff to help.

Across the state, families said goodbye to sons, brothers, and husbands. Also in Raleigh, U.S. Sen. Josiah W. Bailey's 24-year-old son James wired the Selective Service saying he wished to resign his job with the Federal Bureau of Investigation to join the Army. Seventeen-year-old William S. Hinton of Wilson finally gained the quarter-inch he needed to meet the Marines' 5-foot-4 minimum height rule by hanging from a chinning bar for hours on end. Standing straight and tall William was sworn in December 11 while his parents looked on.

FIRST IN FLIGHT In May 1942, cadets begin arriving on the campus of the University of North Carolina at Chapel Hill to train as pilots at the Navy's Pre-Flight School.

BASIC TRAINING

The enormity of the government's commitment to military preparedness actually hit home in North Carolina beginning in 1941. An extensive network of bases and training sites quickly sprang up, the War Department taking advantage of the state's vast tracts of flat land and open skies close to the coast.

At Fort Bragg, a nine-month construction blitz transformed the World War I artillery training camp and its Pope airfield into one of the largest military complexes in the country. Nearly simultaneously, the Marine Corps opened its amphibious training base, Camp Lejeune. Months later, the Corps commissioned the Cherry Point air station to train pilots for Pacific duty.

Fort Bragg and Camp Lejeune were the largest bases in the state, but many more were on the way. Camp Mackall was built to train paratroopers. Laurinburg-Maxton Army Air Base specialized in glider pilots. Camp Davis drilled anti-aircraft artillery crews. To protect vital supply convoys while hunting enemy submarines, the Navy opened air stations at Ocracoke, Manteo, and Elizabeth City, and the Marines established an air station at Edenton.

In cities large enough to have airports, the military moved in and made them bigger. The Army Air Forces took over municipal airports at Charlotte, Winston-Salem, Greensboro, Raleigh-Durham, and Wilmington. Goldsboro's Seymour Johnson Airport, just opened in December 1941, became the training base for P-47 Thunderbolt fighter pilots.

By 1943, North Carolina was training more troops than any other state; the total would reach more than 2 million by war's end.

— *David La Vere*

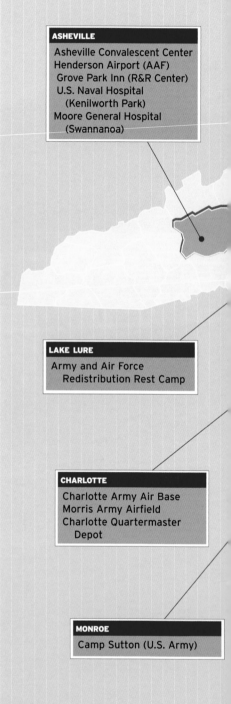

ASHEVILLE
Asheville Convalescent Center
Henderson Airport (AAF)
Grove Park Inn (R&R Center)
U.S. Naval Hospital
 (Kenilworth Park)
Moore General Hospital
 (Swannanoa)

LAKE LURE
Army and Air Force
 Redistribution Rest Camp

CHARLOTTE
Charlotte Army Air Base
Morris Army Airfield
Charlotte Quartermaster
 Depot

MONROE
Camp Sutton (U.S. Army)

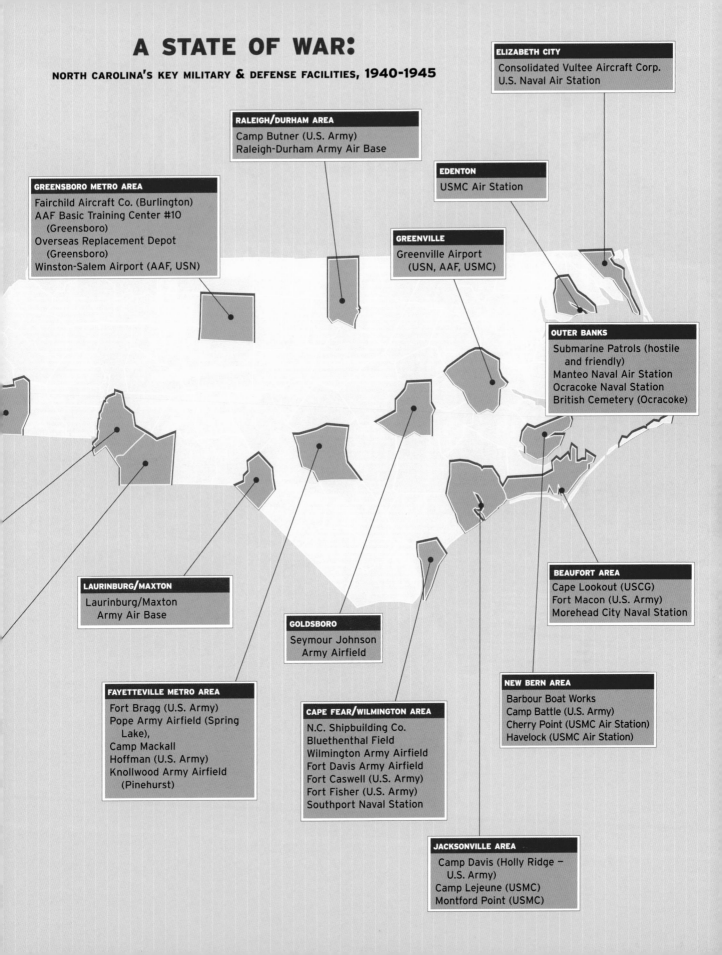

A STATE OF WAR:

NORTH CAROLINA'S KEY MILITARY & DEFENSE FACILITIES, 1940-1945

ELIZABETH CITY
Consolidated Vultee Aircraft Corp.
U.S. Naval Air Station

RALEIGH/DURHAM AREA
Camp Butner (U.S. Army)
Raleigh-Durham Army Air Base

EDENTON
USMC Air Station

GREENSBORO METRO AREA
Fairchild Aircraft Co. (Burlington)
AAF Basic Training Center #10
   (Greensboro)
Overseas Replacement Depot
   (Greensboro)
Winston-Salem Airport (AAF, USN)

GREENVILLE
Greenville Airport
   (USN, AAF, USMC)

OUTER BANKS
Submarine Patrols (hostile
   and friendly)
Manteo Naval Air Station
Ocracoke Naval Station
British Cemetery (Ocracoke)

LAURINBURG/MAXTON
Laurinburg/Maxton
   Army Air Base

GOLDSBORO
Seymour Johnson
Army Airfield

BEAUFORT AREA
Cape Lookout (USCG)
Fort Macon (U.S. Army)
Morehead City Naval Station

FAYETTEVILLE METRO AREA
Fort Bragg (U.S. Army)
Pope Army Airfield (Spring
   Lake),
Camp Mackall
Hoffman (U.S. Army)
Knollwood Army Airfield
   (Pinehurst)

CAPE FEAR/WILMINGTON AREA
N.C. Shipbuilding Co.
Bluethenthal Field
Wilmington Army Airfield
Fort Davis Army Airfield
Fort Caswell (U.S. Army)
Fort Fisher (U.S. Army)
Southport Naval Station

NEW BERN AREA
Barbour Boat Works
Camp Battle (U.S. Army)
Cherry Point (USMC Air Station)
Havelock (USMC Air Station)

JACKSONVILLE AREA
Camp Davis (Holly Ridge –
   U.S. Army)
Camp Lejeune (USMC)
Montford Point (USMC)

THE GREAT CAROLINA MANEUVERS

The U.S. Army converged on the Carolinas in late 1941 for a last great peacetime test of its ground forces. Commanded by Generals Patton, Drum, McNair, and Marshall, hundreds of thousands of troops took part in the large-scale war games, the point being to find out whether tanks could hold their ground against anti-tank weaponry. Here, the tanks lost. The maneuvers concluded a week before the attack on Pearl Harbor.

"OLD BLOOD AND GUTS"

Gen. Omar Bradley, who both served under and commanded Gen. George Patton, described him as "the strangest duck I have ever known." North Carolina farm girl Linda McIntyre made a similar assessment when she encountered the general by chance when Patton's troops were camped on her family's Union County farm during the Carolina Maneuvers. "He was a loud and blustery fellow, wearing his white gloves and hat. He was something different than I had ever seen before. I was astounded by him."

NATIONAL ARCHIVES

GENERAL GREATNESS American generals, seated left to right, are William H. Simpson, George S. Patton Jr., Carl Spaatz, Dwight D. Eisenhower, Omar Bradley, Courtney H. Hodges, and Leonard T. Gerow; standing, from left to right, are Ralph F. Stearley, Hoyt S. Vandenberg, Walter Bedell Smith, Otto P. Weyland, and Richard E. Nugent.

A BRIDGE TOO FAR Cpl. Shuler Eugene Harman places dynamite to demolish a bridge at Fort Bragg *(left)* during training maneuvers in 1941.

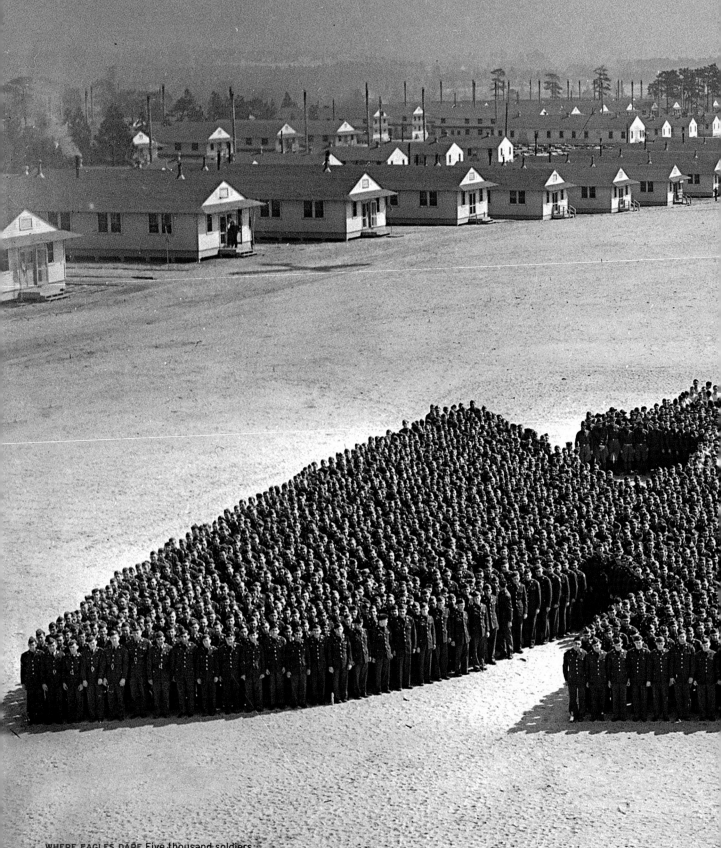

WHERE EAGLES DARE Five thousand soldiers stand in perfect formation on Army Day – April 6, 1942 – at Fort Bragg, the nation's largest Army camp.

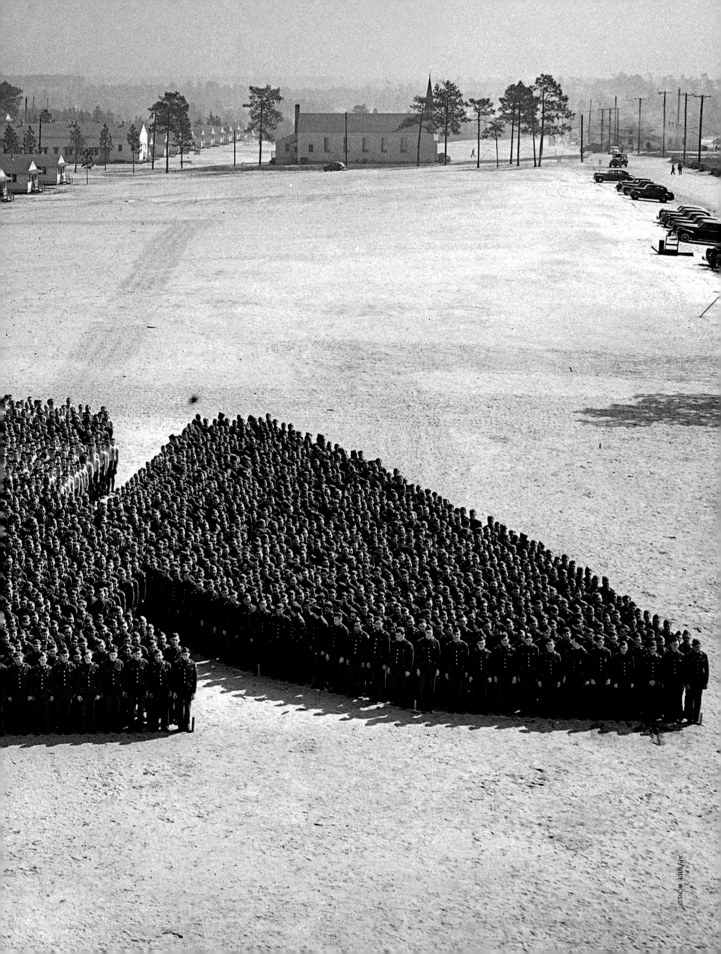

BIG AS A BLIMP At Camp Davis, North Carolina's first barrage balloon training facility, U.S. Army and British forces practice using balloons to battle German air raids. Also known as "Camp Swampy," the station in the coastal town of Holly Ridge operates as the only post to train troops in anti-aircraft, seacoast defense, and barrage balloons under one command.

HUGH MORTON

DRESSED FOR SUCCESS

If you're worried about the soldiers on maneuvers not having any Thanksgiving dinner this year, just forget all your anxieties. According to the quartermaster subsistence office, soldiers at Fort Bragg will consume some 24,000 pounds of turkey. As the birds weigh anywhere from eight to 20 pounds each, it is estimated that the number of gobblers to receive military funerals on November 20 will approximate 1,600.

— The State: A Weekly Survey of North Carolina, *November, 22, 1941*

THE POET'S CORNER

Marines at Camp Lejeune are turning very poetic these days. In order to stimulate interest in the Fourth War Loan, furloughs of from two to five days are being awarded for the best jingles submitted dealing with the campaign. Women Marines are expected to walk off with the awards, but Capt. Harold J. Fox, camp auditor and war bond officer, says, "They've got more poetry in their souls."

— The State: A Weekly Survey of North Carolina, *January 29, 1944*

VOICES CARRY

Recently a new lieutenant was assigned to a company at Camp Mackall and his small stature and fragile appearance caused many audible comments from the men, among them being a booming voice saying, "and a little child shall lead them." The next morning, on the bulletin board where all announcements are made, the following notice appeared: "The company will take a 25-mile hike today with a full pack — and a little child shall lead them."

— The State: A Weekly Survey of North Carolina, *February 26, 1944*

BOW WOW BOOT CAMP

The first canine "Devil Dogs" enlisted in military service only little more than a year ago but already proving valuable in the Pacific Theater were trained at Camp Lejeune. ... For the first time in American annals, a trained war dog unit landed with Marines on Bougainville Island, last major Japanese stronghold in the Solomons, and immediately lived up to the Leatherneck motto "Always Faithful."

Six of the 24 dogs were officially cited for bravery. ... Caesar, a strapping, three-year-old German shepherd trained as a messenger, became the only means of communication between "M" Company and headquarters. For two days and nights he slipped through enemy fire and carried messages and maps. On the third night he sprang from a foxhole just in time to prevent a Japanese soldier from throwing a hand grenade.

— The State: A Weekly Survey of North Carolina, *July 1, 1944*

BOTH IMAGES: U.S. MARINE CORPS

THE FEW. THE PROUD. THE FIRST.

At President Roosevelt's directive, the Marine Corps broke with tradition and opened its ranks to African-Americans in August 1942, but trained them at a separate boot camp on the fringes of Camp Lejeune. The Montford Point Leathernecks went on to serve in segregated defense battalions and combat support companies and fought in some of the war's bloodiest campaigns. After Marines subdued Japanese forces on Saipan, Corps Commander Alexander Vandegrift declared: "The Negro Marines are no longer on trial. They are Marines, period."

A FEW GOOD MEN In 1942, two young men who would become U.S. presidents served part of their time in the Armed Forces at the U.S. Navy's Pre-Flight Training School at the University of North Carolina at Chapel Hill. George Bush *(above, center)* volunteered for service on his 18th birthday and fought in the Pacific after completing the 10-month course. Gerald Ford *(right, wearing solid trunks)* worked as one of the program's 83 instructors.

JEEPS AT THE POST MOTOR POOL, Camp Butner, N. C.

BUILDING BOOM

In rapid-fire fashion, the Army took just six months in 1942 to complete Camp Butner and begin using the 40,000-acre site north of Durham to train infantry troops, including artillery and engineering units. The soldiers trained on about 15 different firing ranges, including a grenade range and flamethrower practice pad. A mock German village was also erected for shooting practice. The base was home to one of the Army's largest hospitals as well, and the War Department's Army Redeployment Center. In September 1943, Butner began interning German prisoners of war (*shown above*).

SO CLOSE, YET SO FAR AWAY

"Finally, on a cold, rainy night, the train stopped. An officer, who I had never seen, came to our section and told us we were in Camp Butner, North Carolina, and we would be stationed there. I had never heard of Camp Butner and neither had anyone else. Bag and baggage, we were loaded on a G.I. truck and hauled to a barracks. It was daylight now. I remember looking out the window and all I could see was red mud. I was never so surprised to learn that we were in or near Durham. It was here that 13 weeks of basic training began. At the end of this 13 weeks, I was promoted to private first class. All who were not promoted were shipped overseas, and we were left to train the next bunch of greenhorns."

— *Will Best, Greensboro, Stumpy Point, U.S. Army*

ARMY TOWN

Nearly 90,000 Army Air Forces recruits received their basic training in Greensboro, at one of the rare military camps entirely within a city. The base opened in March 1943 north of downtown on 650 acres leased from Cone Mills. Little more than a year later, reflecting the military's more pressing need to reassign soldiers rather than train them, the base became a major overseas replacement depot. About 330,000 soldiers got their marching orders in Greensboro through the duration of the war.

For 20-year-old Pvt. Charlton Heston, the highlight of his basic training at Greensboro was his impromptu wedding to Lydia Clarke on March 17, 1944. According to Jeff Thigpen, Guilford County Register of Deeds, Heston's autographed marriage certificate still hangs on the wall of the Vital Records office.

STREET FIGHTING MEN On September 24, 1943, soldiers from Camp Butner and Greensboro's Basic Training Center #10 invade the Gate City with Jeeps, half-tracks, and all types of weapons. The military exercise includes house-to-house fighting and the capture of vital installations, such as city hall and the telegraph office.

Back to Work

Defense contracts poured more than $2 billion into North Carolina, a welcome jolt of pocket money for an economy long starved by the Great Depression.

"Every man in the armed service of the United States," said Gov. J. Melville Broughton in 1944, "has some article made in North Carolina." In addition to towels, bandages, and camouflage cloth, Cannon Mills in Kannapolis supplied yarn for 15 million machine-gun belts. Forced to curtail its output of women's hosiery due to the nylon shortage, the P.H. Hanes Knitting Co. in Winston-Salem instead kept its 3,300 workers busy producing underwear for the military. The Edwards machine shop in Sanford supplied hydraulics for military aircraft. A large artillery shell plant opened on Charlotte's southern edge in January 1943. The hard-working men and women led 28 North Carolina companies to receive the Army-Navy "E" Production Award, the highest recognition given in war production plants.

High-school students and POWs helped make up for the scarcity of farm workers, allowing the state to double its wheat production. Tobacco was left in the field until the cotton, hay, and peanuts had been harvested.

POWER STATION Responding to an urgent need for electrical power for war use, the Tennessee Valley Authority accelerated construction of Fontana Dam in the remote North Carolina mountains in 1942. The TVA hired 5,000 laborers to keep the project moving forward around the clock. Cottages and dormitories were built on-site for the workers, and nearly overnight a general store, church, post office, and hospital made it a real town. The 480-foot dam – the tallest east of the Rocky Mountains – was completed in January 1945.

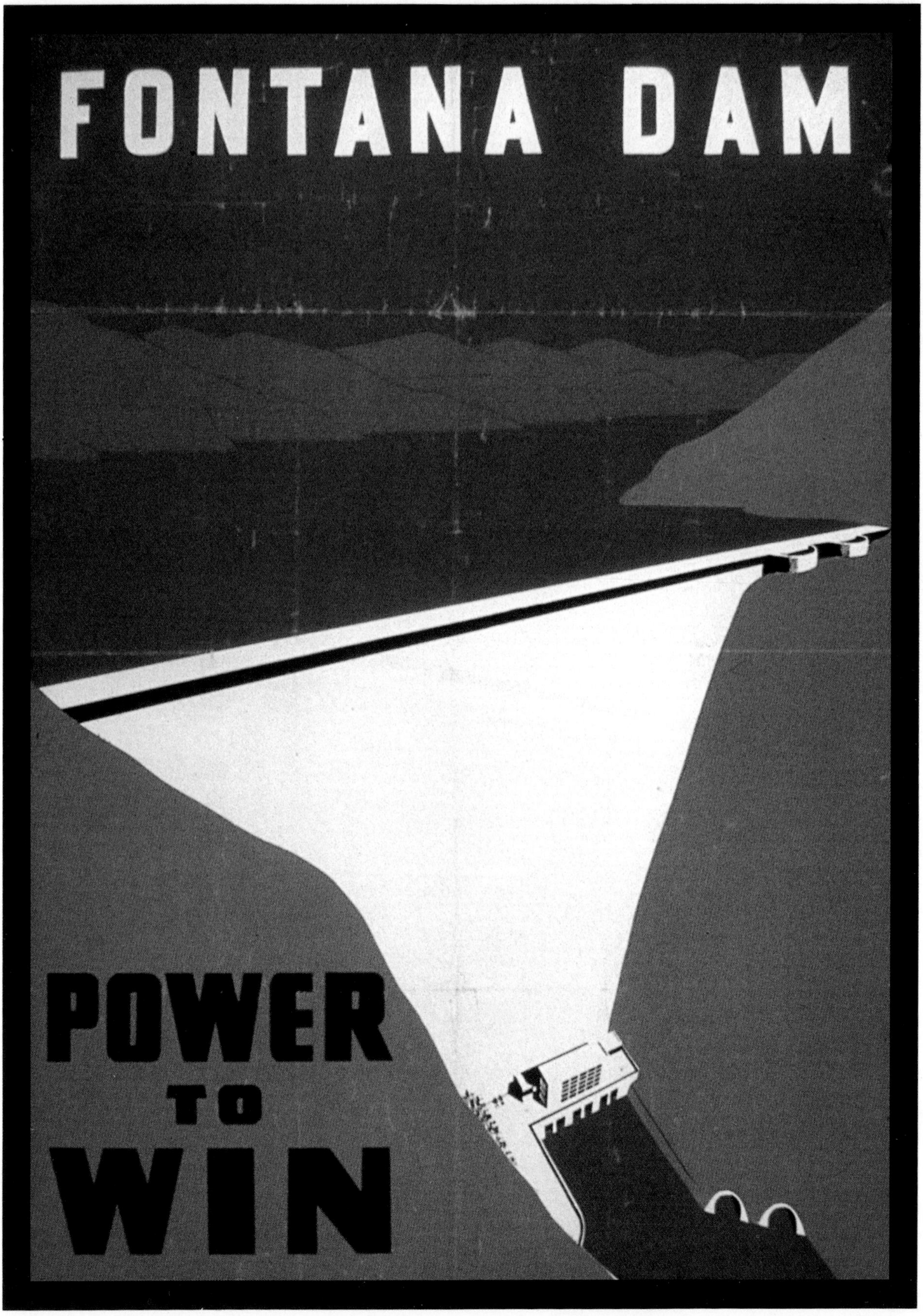
FONTANA DAM
POWER
TO
WIN

PLANE JANES Young women help assemble training aircraft at the Fairchild plant in Burlington.

A STATE OF ROSIES

As the country shifted to wartime production, American women — including many who had never held a job outside the home — made a huge contribution by filling skilled industrial jobs previously done by men. Rosie the Riveter symbolized the strength, courage, and the "we can do it" spirit of these homefront heroes.

HAT'S OFF

You've got to take your hat off to the women of North Carolina — they did their share during the war. War Manpower Commissioner J.S. Dorton said this week that women composed half of the labor force in the Tar Heel State during the peak of war production.

— The State: A Weekly Survey of North Carolina, *September 22, 1945*

A CHANGE OF PLANS

"During the school year 1943-1944, I attended Meredith College in Raleigh. But with the war raging, I began to think I should help the effort, so during the summer of 1944 I worked at a war plant in Winston-Salem called National Carbon Company. We did not know what we were making; the product was not finished there, and it was only a part of something. We found out after the war that it was for the Navy.

"At the end of that summer I joined the Cadet Nurses Corps and attended St. Leo's Hospital in Greensboro for training. My mother wasn't real happy with my choice, but it was my choice and I had to make it. It was just the right thing to do.

"When Germany surrendered in May 1945, I realized the war would be over soon, so I decided to return to college to complete my degree.

"I worked at National Carbon again during the summer of 1945. On August 14, I was preparing to go to work on the second shift when word came that Japan had surrendered. We didn't have to go to work that day. Our work was finished."

— *Frances Simpson Best, Stokesdale*

BETH LYKES

SHIP SHAPE

Liberty ships were "built by the mile and chopped off by the yard," so the saying went, a nod to the almost assembly-line efficiency with which the North Carolina Shipbuilding Co. and 17 other yards were turning out the cargo vessels. At its peak, the Wilmington yard had the best productivity of any of the Liberty builders, launching a complete ship in a month. So many were being worked on side by side in the nine shipways, "you could literally step from one to the other without touching the water for miles," a Wilmington resident remembers. North Carolina Shipbuilding delivered 126 Liberty ships and 117 Victory ships from 1941 to 1946.

UGLY DUCKLINGS GO TO WAR "Admiral, I think this ship will do us very well," President Roosevelt said when shown plans in early 1941 for a cargo vessel that would become the Liberty ship. "She isn't much to look at though, is she? A real ugly duckling." Under its prefabricated and welded skin, the beauty of the uncomplicated vessel shone in its sturdy reliability and the fact that one could be completed in just weeks instead of months for about $1.5 million apiece. A slow ship with an expected life of five years at most, the Liberty greatly exceeded expectations by convoying food, war materials, and troops to England, Africa, and the islands of the Pacific throughout the war with a loss of only 200 of the 2,710 that were launched.

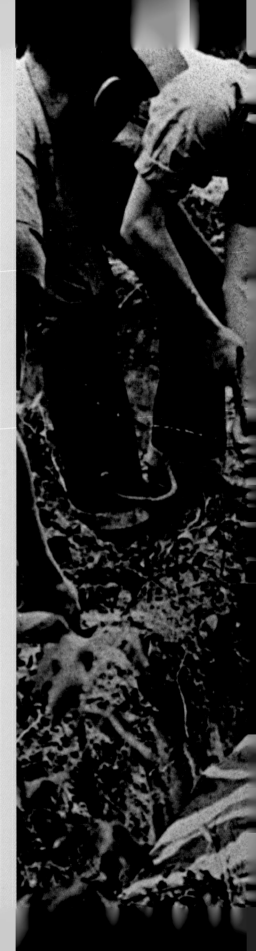

TORPEDO JUNCTION

While U.S. troops headed overseas to fight in early 1942, German U-boats brought the war to America's front door — and were astonished to find it still wide open despite the declaration of war.

Where the enemy submariners expected coastal defenses and resistance, they found easy pickings. Freighters and tankers continued to travel as they had in peacetime — usually alone and alit. Their wreckage washed ashore with terrifying regularity over the first six months of the year.

"In time of war, you put your best foot forward," said historian and former Navy Intelligence officer Gordon Vaeth on PBS's "Nova: Hitler's Lost Sub." "The Navy was saying, 'Don't worry, we're taking care of these submarines, we're sinking them.' In actuality, we hadn't sunk a single one."

The U-boat swarms found their greatest satisfaction off the Outer Banks, where Cape Hatteras served as a navigational focal point. There was so much destruction here that the area became known as "Torpedo Junction."

Organized convoys, anti-submarine patrols, and coastal blackouts began to turn the tide in May of 1942; by mid-July the U-boats were gone. The bloodbath of Torpedo Junction was finally a closed chapter, but in its wake were 397 sunken ships, some 80 of them in North Carolina waters.

— *David La Vere*

FOREVER ENGLAND

The HMS *Bedfordshire*, one of two dozen British anti-submarine trawlers lent to the U.S. Navy for coastal patrol and convoy duty, became a victim itself of a prowling German U-boat on May 11, 1942, off Cape Lookout. On a piece of land donated by Alice Wahab Williams next to her own family's cemetery on Ocracoke, the bodies of four sailors recovered near the island were laid to rest. A "foreign field" at the time, the tiny gravesite was later deeded to Great Britain.

SECRETS OF THE DEEP U-85's reign of terror abruptly ends when the USS *Roper* shells the sub off the coast of Bodie Island on April 14, 1942 — the first U-boat sunk off the East Coast. In 2001, divers recovered the sub's "Enigma" machine, which allowed German Admiral Karl Dönitz to command his underwater wolf pack fleet. It is now housed at the Graveyard of the Atlantic Museum on Hatteras Island.

WATER TORTURE Richard Rushton, just 18, was making his maiden voyage aboard the *Dixie Arrow* on March 26, 1942, when a U-boat torpedo ignited and sank the tanker near Ocracoke, killing 33 crewmen. "It was a pleasant life on merchant ships, but it didn't seem to be a safe occupation, being torpedoed on my very first trip," Rushton remarked later. "So I joined the Navy."

CHAPTER THREE

COURAGE

COMBATING AN AXIS OF ENEMIES

"You ask, what is our aim? ... It is victory, victory
at all costs, victory in spite of all terror, victory
however long and hard the road may be; for
without victory, there is no survival."

— *Winston Churchill, May 14, 1940, before British House of Commons*

SHELL SHOCKED Watchful of enemy snipers, soldiers of the 30th Infantry Division maneuver their way through the French town of Mortain in August 1944. Known as the "Workhorse of the Western Front," the division counted many North Carolinians in its ranks.

1778   1943

AMERICANS
will __always__ fight for liberty

War Against Fascism

By the autumn of 1942, Axis powers occupied most of continental Europe, North Africa, and the Middle East. They had invaded the Soviet Union, kept up the bombardment of Great Britain, and wreaked havoc in the Atlantic. Fascist ambition seemed boundless. But the tide was turning, and North Carolina was doing its part to stanch enemy advancement. Preparation at N.C. training facilities proved invincible as native North Carolinians and those stationed here helped drive Nazi forces from the beaches of Normandy to Berlin. To the south, Benito Mussolini suffered a similar defeat in North Africa.

THE FACE OF APPEASEMENT
Resigned to Nazi occupation, a grief-stricken Czech woman salutes as Hitler claims the Sudetenland in September 1938.

A FLYING FORTRESS

U.S. Army Air Forces Col. Robert K. Morgan of Asheville became one of the most celebrated heroes of the war as the pilot of the *Memphis Belle* — a B-17 he named in honor of one-time sweetheart Margaret Polk of Memphis. Morgan piloted the first American bomber to complete 25 daytime missions over occupied Europe between November 7, 1942 and May 17, 1943. Morgan received the Distinguished Flying Cross with two Oak Leaf Clusters and the Air Medal with 10 Oak Leaf Clusters.

Following a public relations tour in the United States, Morgan resumed flying in 1944 as a bomber pilot and completed 26 missions over Japan. The B-29, *Dauntless Dotty*, he named after his bride, Dorothy.

MISSIONS ACCOMPLISHED Robert Morgan *(above, sixth from left)* and the crew of the *Memphis Belle* receive heroes' welcomes at an air base in England after completing their 25th European mission in the spring of 1943. The famous bomber pilot receives the Distinguished Flying Cross from Brig. Gen. H.S. Hansell *(left)*.

A RED-TAILED ANGEL

The B-17 was in trouble — shot up, alone over Germany, and with a string of enemy fighters closing in — when four American P-51 Mustang fighters suddenly flashed out of the sun. The Mustangs, their tails painted blood red, downed all four fighters and escorted the bomber to a base in Italy. Wanting to thank the "red-tailed angels" who saved them, the bomber crew strolled over to the 99th Fighter Squadron, then stopped in surprise: The squadron was an all-black unit known as the Tuskegee Airmen. "They couldn't believe it. Called us liars," said Wilson Eagleson.

Trained in Tuskegee, Alabama, the Durham native joined the 99th at Tunisia in September 1943. "We were trained as bomber escorts, but white commanders didn't let us do it. … So they assigned us the dirty work of dive-bombing and strafing German troops. We did that until July 4, 1944, when we got our first P-51 Mustangs." In Italy, "we shot down 12 German FW-190s on one day. I got one that day in September." After the rescue of the B-17, "we began to get missions to escort bombers. The bomber crews realized we were pretty good, too; they gave us our nickname — Red-Tailed Angels."

— *David La Vere*

THE SKY'S THE LIMIT First Lt. Wilson Eagleson (*above*), one of the famed Tuskegee Airmen, flew 362 missions and shot down at least two German fighter planes.

SHOOTING THE BREEZE Fliers of a P-51 Mustang Group (*right*) in Italy kneel in the shadow of one of the Mustangs they fly.

The News and Observer

INVASION OF EUROPE BEGINS

Montgomery Leads Allied Force Landing On French North Coast

Roosevelt Hails Fall of Rome, But Warns of Hard Job Ahead

HELPING TURN THE TIDE AT NORMANDY

Fourteen-year-old Jack Hoffler of Hertford enlisted in the Navy in August 1943. His sister forged their mother's signature for him, lying about his age. "My mother didn't care if I went, but she wouldn't lie."

Hoffler became the youngest combat sailor on D-Day. Assigned to a landing craft that carried troops and supplies ashore on Omaha Beach and ferried wounded back to the ship, his job was to drop the bow ramp. "It was solid chaos and just a helluva mess. The minute those troops started running out there, machine guns would open up right in front of me, killing half of them before they got off the boat. I'm lucky I didn't get killed myself."

Each time, he jumped out on the ramp, pulled dead and wounded men off, then cranked the craft back up to retrieve more troops. He made more than a dozen trips on June 6 and started over again on June 7. That night, his boat hit a mine and sank, but he and another sailor made it to the beach. He remained there more than a month. Though wounded in the throat, Hoffler never received a Purple Heart. Because he was too young to enlist, he didn't qualify.

— *Jimmy Tomlin*

FATHER OF THE AIRBORNE

As paratroopers jumped into the dark morning hours of June 6, 1944, they yelled the name of their former commander — the architect of their mission — "Bill Lee!" Such was their admiration for the "Father of the Airborne."

Lee had been an infantry officer during World War I, then served as a military attaché in France and Britain. During the 1930s, he saw the success of Germany's airborne unit and began lobbying his superiors to create an American airborne unit.

"They basically told him to shut up," said Keith Finch, board member of the Gen. William C. Lee Museum in Lee's hometown of Dunn. "But he kept on talking about it, and then President Roosevelt decided we needed to investigate forming some airborne troops, and he was asked to do it."

Lee set about establishing the unit initially at Fort Benning, Georgia, and then at Fort Bragg. In August 1942, he became the first commanding general of the 101st Airborne Division, the "Screaming Eagles."

"Lee was in on the planning of the D-Day invasion — he did a lot of the planning for the airborne drop," said Finch. "But in February of '44, he had a heart attack. He had another minor heart attack in April, so they sent him home around May."

That was probably one of Lee's greatest disappointments — having to listen to the D-Day attack on a radio, rather than be there himself. That's why paratroopers of the 101st shouted their beloved former commander's name over the skies of France.

— *Jimmy Tomlin*

SOLDIERS IN THE SKY Clockwise from top left: In August 1942, Gen. Bill Lee becomes the first to lead the "Screaming Eagles"; Lee inspects Army paratroopers; Lee in his paratrooper gear; the Harnett County native narrates events to Prime Minister Churchill during training exercises in the Carolinas; Fort Bragg paratroopers board a plane for their next mission.

On his first birthday, William C. Price Jr. of Shelby received this letter from his father, a soldier fighting in Italy.

Dear Son:

I haven't as yet had the chance to really be a dad to you; what I mean, son, is that I haven't rocked you to sleep nights, didn't stay up nights with you, haven't been with you when you were sick, when you needed me; I didn't go out and buy things for you like a father does. You see, son, I don't really know how it feels to be a pop, as I have been away from home all this time, doing my share on a job that thousands of other little boys' fathers are also working at, trying to bring peace to the world so that you and all the other little boys can grow up into a world that will never bring the horrors and hardships of war upon your shoulders as it has on the shoulders of us men, who have had to leave our homes and loved ones to fight.

— The State: A Weekly Survey of North Carolina,
January 22, 1944

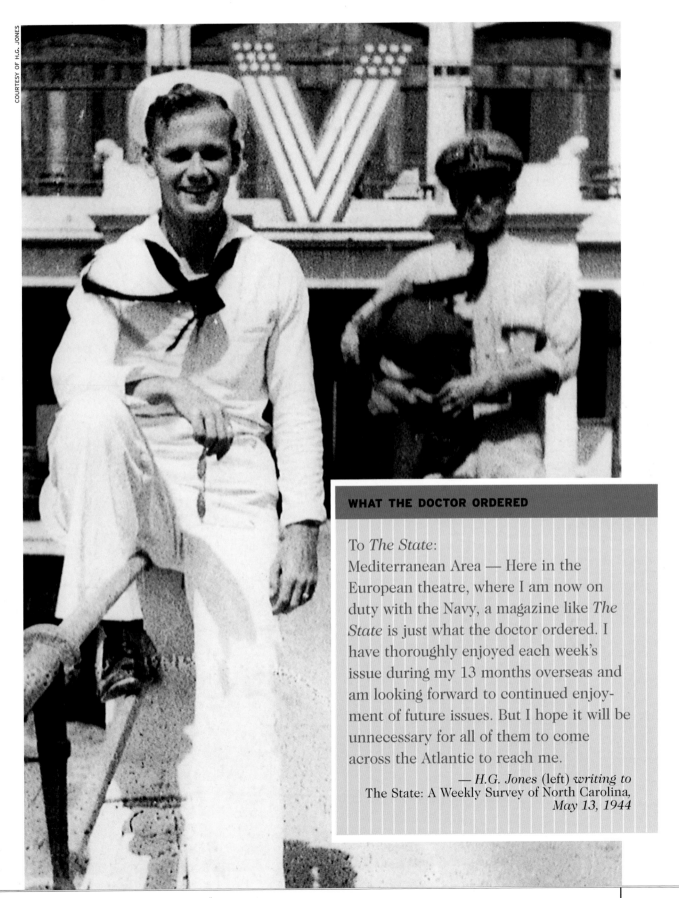

WHAT THE DOCTOR ORDERED

To *The State*:

Mediterranean Area — Here in the European theatre, where I am now on duty with the Navy, a magazine like *The State* is just what the doctor ordered. I have thoroughly enjoyed each week's issue during my 13 months overseas and am looking forward to continued enjoyment of future issues. But I hope it will be unnecessary for all of them to come across the Atlantic to reach me.

— *H.G. Jones* (left) *writing to*
The State: A Weekly Survey of North Carolina,
May 13, 1944

"MINKA"

J.R. Holden of Greensboro finds his new best friend Minka in an old barn while behind German lines. When the war ended, the inseparable companions both return to North Carolina safely.

Reidsville native Raymond Wagoner of the 5th Army's 687th Ammo Co. escapes injury after live ordnance explodes while being unloaded in southeast Italy in 1945. His truck isn't so fortunate.

Norwood Dorman of Benson stops to rest next to a statuesque comrade in Brolo, Sicily.

Eight Forest City area soldiers reunite while en route to the European Theater.

THE PACIFIC THEATER
Defeating the Japanese Empire

On the other side of the globe, North Carolinians joined in the nation's 45-month struggle to end aggression in the Pacific. Employing a island-hopping strategy, American sea, land, and air power began reclaiming occupied lands in the spring of 1942. By the spring of 1945, the question facing the United States was not one of victory, but of the conditions under which the Japanese would surrender. On June 17, 1945, President Harry S. Truman wrote in his diary, "I have to decide Japanese strategy — shall we invade Japan proper or shall we bomb and blockade? That is my hardest decision to date. But I'll make it when I have all the facts."

D-DAY OF THE PACIFIC Japanese snipers take aim at the 4th Marine Division as members rush ashore during the invasion of Saipan in the Mariana Islands in June 1944.

PRIDE OF THE FLEET

Considered the most powerful warship afloat in the world, the USS *North Carolina* symbolized the determination of the American people to win the war against Japan. State of the art in design and technology, she grandly reported for duty in the Pacific in the summer of 1942, two years after being launched from the Brooklyn Navy Yard. Envious sailors on other ships dubbed the classy newcomer "The Showboat," a nickname forever after carried with pride.

The *North Carolina*'s 2,200 sailors and officers saw action in every major naval offensive in the Pacific, proving vital to the Navy's island-hopping campaign that began with the landing of Marines on Guadalcanal in August 1942. She helped establish the two primary roles of the fast battleships — protecting aircraft carriers from air attack and supporting troops ashore.

A Japanese torpedo temporarily put the *North Carolina* out of service in the fall of 1942, but after repairs at Pearl Harbor she went back to sea and spent much of 1943 in the Solomon Islands. In 1945, the ship's formidable firepower helped pave the way for the invasion of Iwo Jima.

Among the many amazing stories that gild the legend of the *North Carolina* was one involving the rescue of downed American flyers during airstrikes in the Caroline Islands in April 1944. In a single morning, the pilot of one of the ship's Kingfisher seaplanes, Lt. John Burns, plucked seven airmen from the heavy seas. Unable to take off with so much weight, he retrieved them and kept everyone afloat until a submarine could pick them up. "The Showboat" became the most decorated American battleship of the war, earning 15 battle stars. She served to war's end, losing 10 of her men in battle.

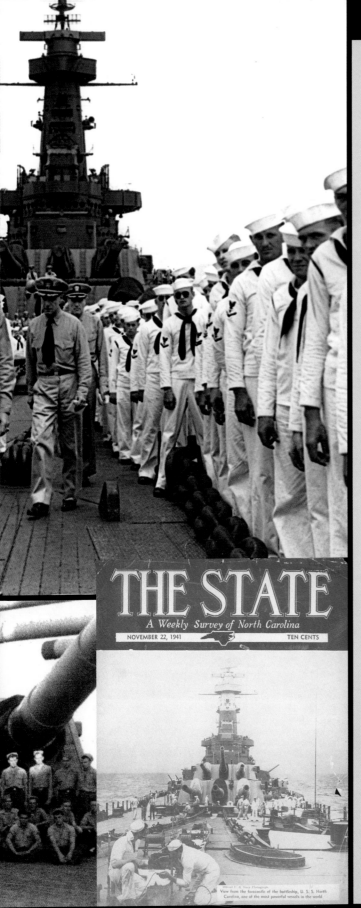

FRIENDLY FIRE

"I was manning a radio position. We had been firing for several minutes, when all of a sudden I heard this loud bang and a large black cloud of smoke enveloped the tower. Instantly, I heard what sounded like someone throwing a handful of marbles against the tower. I was sitting inside but saw one guy fall over. I ran out thinking a bomb had hit us.

"Down on deck men were lying everywhere. Blood was running across the deck. I then saw the hole in the director base and it was obvious a five-inch gun had hit us from one of our own ships. It was a miracle that more of us were not hurt in those close quarters. Three men were killed and 40 were wounded."

— *Charles Paty, Charlotte, U.S. Navy, onboard the* North Carolina *in April 1945 during the Battle of Okinawa*

THE SHOWBOAT Clockwise from top left: Even during wartime, protocoi remains the order of the day during the changing of the guard aboard the *North Carolina*; the ship's massive guns dwarf Paty and crewmates; just weeks before Pearl Harbor, the *North Carolina* appears on the cover of *The State*.

PERILS OF THE PACIFIC Under heavy attack from kamikaze pilots, the *North Carolina* shoots down at least three suicide planes during the 40-day Battle of Okinawa in the spring of 1945.

BATAAN DEATH MARCH Japanese troops force more than 70,000 American and Filipino soldiers to march more than 60 miles to prisoner-of-war camps. Nearly 10,000 die along the way. Bataan is recaptured by the Allies in February 1945.

PARADE OF THE DEAD

Lt. John Bumgarner, a physician with the U.S. Army Medical Corps, had been serving in the Philippines for a little more than a year when the Japanese drove Allied forces from the island's Bataan Peninsula — one of the worst defeats ever suffered by the United States — on April 9, 1942. A native of Wilkes County, Bumgarner was a prisoner of war until the Japanese surrender in 1945.

Lacking medical supplies, suffering from disease and malnutrition, and witnessing harrowing atrocities, the young doctor tried to care for the thousands of American and Filipino soldiers who were forced to march north out of Bataan to Camp O'Donnell, where they were held in captivity. "Death from a bullet," Bumgarner said in his memoir *Parade of the Dead*, "would have been preferable to the desolate and hopeless circumstances which overcame hundreds of others. ... By the middle of June [1942] the grisly procession of dead had grown alarmingly to average 20 deaths per day — 20 men who had endured the terrible ordeal of Bataan, who were 10,000 miles from home, and who then died in the most miserable circumstances. For me, as a doctor, the most distressing thought was that they could have been saved, almost without exception, by proper diet and medical care."

— *Diane Silcox-Jarrett*

A SOBERING EXPERIENCE

William H. Wood *(above, right)* was pumping gas at the O.R. Neighbor's Curb Market on Main Street in High Point when he heard the news out of Pearl Harbor. Only 16, he knew he wanted to fight for his country but it took a year to persuade his parents. They finally let him sign up for the Navy after extracting a promise not to drink any alcohol when he went off to enlist.

The young teetotaler happily agreed, and he along with six other High Point youths joined the 7th Fleet aboard the USS *Los Angeles* on December 26, 1944. He served two and a half years in the South Pacific, returning home quite sober — not only from the promise he kept to his parents but also from the sights he witnessed during the war.

— *Amy Jo Wood*

Louis R. Kittel

YAMAMOTO'S LAST FLIGHT

On April 18, 1943, Lt. Gordon Whittiker of Selma *(bottom right kneeling)* was one of the elite pilots of the 339th Fighter Squadron that departed from Guadacanal on "Operation Vengeance" — a secret mission to down the transport carrying Admiral Isoroku Yamamoto. Having deciphered the Japanese naval code, the U.S. Army Air Forces learned the Japanese architect of the assault on Pearl Harbor had scheduled an inspection tour in the Northern Solomon Islands. The U.S. military quickly devised the plan, and on April 18, 1943, the aerial ambush succeeded after only four minutes. Two bursts of gunfire struck the plane, and it crashed into the jungle.

COURTESY OF TOM COLONES

WAR IS HELL

A member of the 4th Marine Division deployed in the Pacific, Everett "Bud" Hampton (*front row, third from the left*) of Kannapolis faced the reality of war at 8:04 a.m. on June 15, 1944. "That was my first minute of serious combat as a Marine. I was part of the first wave to go onto Saipan. It was the most shocking and frightful moment of my life up to that time. I have never been able to come up with words to describe what I saw there."

After a gruesome 35 days the battle was over, and Hampton was up for an officer's commission. "I was supposed to have a physical to get the commission but the doctor asked me if I had been on the island since the Saipan D-Day and I told him yes. He said that was good enough."

During the invasion of Iwo Jima, his unit came in as a reserve. "I thought I was prepared for anything. But no one could be prepared for Iwo Jima. Marines were lying everywhere, we knew this was going to be horrible."

The death toll on those beaches was so high, Hampton became the company commander inside a week. "You didn't have time to learn men's names. They would come in as a replacement and be dead before you got to know who they were. I guess I am lucky that I have let myself forget much of what happened."

— *Diane Silcox-Jarrett*

THE FLAG RAISERS

"The first flag that went up [on Mount Suribachi in February 1945] came off the ship I went there on, the USS *Missoula*, and all these guys that put the flag up were on that same ship. Colonel Johnson ordered that the flag be put up there when they took the hill. They put it up [but] the mountain was so high you couldn't see it. He wanted everybody out there on the ships and on the whole island to see it, so he ordered another flag. There was nothing particularly exciting about it. All it meant to us was that we had taken that hill, you know. I never thought it would be a famous picture."

— *Neil "Hector" McNeill, Whiteville, U.S. Navy.*
A combat medic, he followed the first
two waves of Marines ashore at Iwo Jima.

source: Special Collections,
William Madison Randall Library, UNCW

For your country's sake today—

For your own sake tomorrow

GO TO THE NEAREST RECRUITING STATION
OF THE ARMED SERVICE OF YOUR CHOICE

IN SERVICE

Women in Uniform

Across North Carolina, more than 7,000 Tar Heel women joined the Armed Forces, taking on jobs and challenges they would have never had before the war.

Although women were not drafted or permitted to serve in combat, they often volunteered for military service, some working as enlisted personnel and officers, while others trained in such specialized positions as pilots and nurses. And despite the ambivalence they sometimes faced from family, male G.I.s, politicians, and military officials, the women of North Carolina stepped out of their homes and into careers.

WHEN DUTY CALLS WASP pilots Viola Thompson and Mary Clifford return safely from towing targets for anti-aircraft artillery practice at Camp Davis.

AIR POWER

"My parents were not excited when I joined the WASPs," said Dorothy Hoover. Dazzled by Charles Lindbergh as a young girl in Asheville, she grew up with a huge desire to fly.

With 200 hours of flying under her belt, Hoover joined the WASPs at age 24. "My husband was in the South Pacific. I figured there wasn't much he could do about it over there."

Hoover flew C-60s, used to tow invasion gliders like those used on D-Day. Pulling targets for aerial gunnery practice was another part of her job. "I never really thought that someone might miss and hit me. I had confidence in them."

Aware that some male pilots resented the women, Hoover didn't care what they said "as long as they let me fly."

— *Diane Silcox-Jarrett*

JOINING FORCES	
WAC:	WOMEN'S ARMY AUXILIARY CORPS
WASP:	WOMEN AIRFORCE SERVICE PILOTS
WAVE:	WOMEN ACCEPTED FOR VOLUNTEER EMERGENCY SERVICES
SPAR:	*SEMPER PARATUS* – ALWAYS READY

SECOND THOUGHTS

One of the first African-American "women to join the WACs, Millie Veasey of Raleigh had second thoughts after signing up. "I rode the bus to Fayetteville with a friend of mine to take the test. There were 21 of us taking the test and only three of us passed. The next day we had to get our physical. It was that day I thought to myself that maybe I didn't want to do this, but they told me it was too late, that I had already signed on the dotted line."

Army life left strong memories. "I was with the first African-American Women's Unit sent overseas. I rode on a ship for six days and was sick the whole time. I threw up over and over. When I saw England I was shocked, it was so torn up. You could hear fighting all around and see what the bombs had done."

— *Diane Silcox-Jarrett*

IN STEP During Greensboro's WAC Week celebration, the guests of honor proudly march through downtown.

"FIRST AVIATRIX OF THE CAROLINAS"

North Carolina's first licensed female pilot, Mary Webb Nicholson of Greensboro served with the British Air Transport Auxiliary of the Royal Air Force to deliver planes from English factories. She was killed in a crash over Berkshire, England, on May 22, 1943.

Her hometown honored the memory of the local heroine February 12, 1944, by proclaiming Mary Nicholson Day. The *Greensboro Daily News* called for $150,000 in war bonds to be raised to buy an ambulance plane in her name.

A note from R. Stafford Cripps, Minister of Aircraft Production in Millbank, England, read, "The Air Transport Auxiliary is doing work of the greatest importance to our war effort and they can ill spare such officers as your daughter. She had proved herself a valuable officer and pilot and she will be greatly missed by all who knew her."

— *Diane Silcox-Jarrett*

AIN'T MISBEHAVIN'

Barbara Gouge of Hickory stayed state-side while serving in the women's section of the Coast Guard (SPARs), but learned that the military meant business. "The leaders in the Coast Guard were not fooling around. They made sure that we kept on a schedule and followed all the rules. They didn't have time for us not to do what we were supposed to do."

Gouge joined up to help out with the war and make a change in her life. "My mother had died when I was young. I wasn't married and I needed to take charge of my life. I needed to feel I was accomplishing something and not just sitting back not taking an active part. It was the best thing I could have ever done."

— *Diane Silcox-Jarrett*

NO ORDINARY TIME Pilots such as Mary Nelson, a WASP at Camp Davis, followed Eleanor Roosevelt's 1942 call to action: "This is not a time when women should be patient. We are in a war and we need to fight it with all our ability and every weapon possible. Women pilots, in this particular case, are a weapon waiting to be used."

TAR HEEL OF THE WEEK

This honor, without a shadow of a doubt, goes this week to Col. Westray Battle Boyce, formerly of Rocky Mount, who rose up through the commissioned ranks of the Women's Army Corps to finally become its head. The 43-year-old North Carolina woman was in the federal government eight years prior to entering the Army.

— The State: A Weekly Survey of North Carolina, *July 21, 1945*

PIONEERING SPIRIT Appointed as WAC director in July 1945, Col. Westray Battle Boyce oversaw the demobilization of the women's corps after the Japanese surrendered. Three years later, Congress passed legislation giving WAC a permanent place in the U.S. Army.

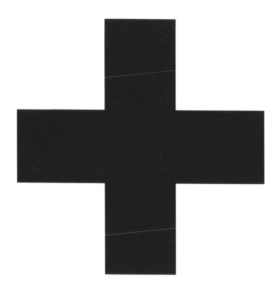

And Their Caretakers

They were a stoic and brave breed, the thousands of North Carolina men and women who were wounded or killed during the war. Many were not old enough to vote, yet they hurt, suffered, and died for their country. And equally as courageous and compassionate were those who cared for the wounded. Many of them had never been far from home — yet, by war's end, they had crossed oceans, cleaned wounds, held the hands of the injured, and heard the last words of the dying.

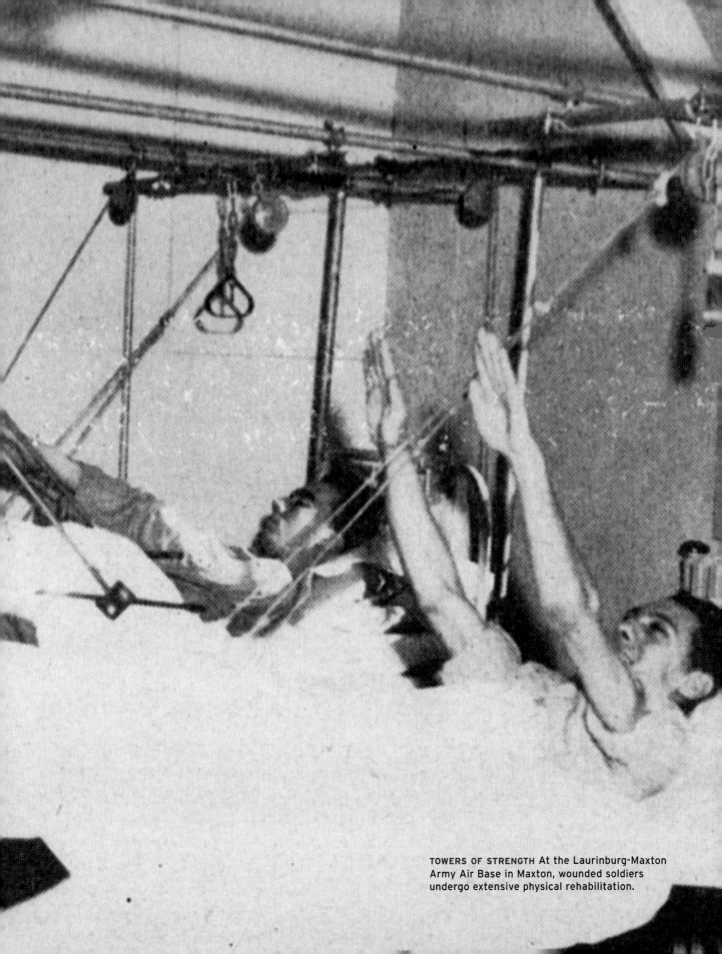

TOWERS OF STRENGTH At the Laurinburg-Maxton Army Air Base in Maxton, wounded soldiers undergo extensive physical rehabilitation.

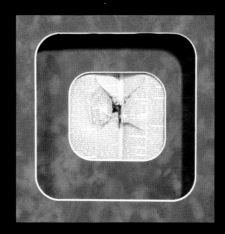

I was drafted into military service in 1943. Before I left for basic training, my aunt gave me a small pocket New Testament with my name inscribed on the front. She asked that I read it daily and carry it in my pocket over my heart, at all times, which I did.

In July 1944, I was sent to France and landed, as a replacement, on Omaha Beach. On November 13, near the French town of Belfourd I was wounded. Snow flurries had fallen all during the day. I was caught out between the lines and hit in the left side of the chest. As I lay there, I was wounded a second time. I lay there for 18 hours during that cold night, listening to the moans and groans from my fellow men. Some crying, some even dying, but I was unable to help. I did a lot of praying during the night.

The next morning I was picked up by litter-bearers and placed on top of a tank while it was being fired at by the enemy. When I arrived at the aid station, my clothes (seven layers, to be exact) and shoes were cut off me and my personal belongings — my wallet and my little Bible — were saved.

After a few days, now coming out from under the drugs, I saw the little Bible and it, too, had taken a hit, by a piece of shrapnel, which had gone through the entire book and was caught in the outer binding of it. That piece of steel would surely have pierced my heart if not my entire body. Little did my wonderful aunt know that this Bible would be a gift of life for me.

— *William Henry "Doc" Long, Summerfield, U.S. Army*

THE GOOD BOOK Doc Long is sure that the New Testament his Aunt May gave him before he departed for Europe saved his life when shrapnel penetrated the book's spine. "I dare say you could take an ice pick, and with all your might have pierced that Bible in its entirety."

To the sweetest mother in all this world loving you Jack

JACKLYN HAROLD LUCAS

Born: February 14, 1928, Plymouth, Washington County
Rank: Private First Class, U.S. Marine Corps Reserve,
1st Battalion, 26th Marines, 5th Marine Division
Location and date: Iwo Jima, Volcano Islands, February 20, 1945

Medal of Honor Citation: "While creeping through a treacherous, twisting ravine which ran in close proximity to a fluid and uncertain frontline on D-plus-1 day, Pfc. Lucas and 3 other men were suddenly ambushed by a hostile patrol which savagely attacked with rifle fire and grenades. Quick to act when the lives of the small group were endangered by 2 grenades which landed directly in front of them, Pfc. Lucas unhesitatingly hurled himself over his comrades upon 1 grenade and pulled the other under him, absorbing the whole blasting forces of the explosions in his own body in order to shield his companions from the concussion and murderous flying fragments. By his inspiring action and valiant spirit of self-sacrifice, he not only protected his comrades from certain injury or possible death but also enabled them to rout the Japanese patrol and continue the advance."

ABOVE AND BEYOND During Jack Lucas's Medal of Honor ceremony, Harry Truman quipped that he would rather be a Medal of Honor winner than president of the United States. "Sir, I'll swap with you," the Marine quickly rejoined as he became the youngest Marine in the 20th century to receive the nation's highest military decoration for bravery.

NORTH CAROLINA WORLD WAR II CONGRESSIONAL MEDAL OF HONOR WINNERS

RAY E. EUBANKS
Awarded posthumously; KIA

Born: February 6, 1922
Snow Hill, Greene County
Rank: Sergeant, U.S. Army,
Company D, 503d Parachute Infantry
Location: Noemfoor Island, Dutch New Guinea, July 23, 1944

WILLIAM DAVID HALYBURTON JR.
Awarded posthumously; KIA

Born: August 2, 1924
Canton, Haywood County
Rank: Pharmacist's Mate Second Class, U.S. Naval Reserve
Location: On Okinawa Shima in the Ryukyu Chain, May 10, 1945

RUFUS G. HERRING
Born: June 11, 1921
Roseboro, Sampson County
Rank: Lieutenant, U.S. Naval Reserve, LCI (G) 449
Location: Iwo Jima, February 17, 1945

MAX THOMPSON
Born: July 21, 1922
Bethel, Pitt County
Rank: Sergeant, U.S. Army,
Company K, 18th Infantry, 1st Infantry Division
Location: Near Haaren, Germany, October 18, 1944

HENRY F. WARNER
Awarded posthumously; KIA

Born: August 23, 1923
Troy, Montgomery County
Rank: Corporal, U.S. Army, Antitank Company, 2d Battalion, 26th Infantry, 1st Infantry Division
Location: Near Dom Butgenbach, Belgium, December 20-21, 1944

source: The U.S. Army:
www.army.mil/cmh-pg/moh1.htm

RETURNING HOME Massachusetts native Harold Russell lost his hands in a grenade explosion while working on an Army film at Camp Mackall on June 6, 1944. Two years later, the veteran won an Academy Award for Best Supporting Actor for his role as Homer Paris – a disabled and disheartened sailor trying to find meaning in postwar America – in *The Best Years of Our Lives.* He also received an honorary Oscar for being an inspiration for disabled veterans.

As if joining the Army Air Corps wasn't adventurous enough, Virginia Reavis of the Onslow County community of Hubert became part of an air evacuation unit. "I was with the 65th General Hospital from Duke University down at Fort Bragg and they were looking for nurses for Air Evac. Only four of us were accepted from Fort Bragg."

Reavis went to Europe in December 1943. "We knew D-Day was coming because they had us flying patients from Europe back to the States, so they could empty out all the beds. It was a sickening feeling knowing what was going to happen. We went in five days after D-Day and took in supplies and loaded up the injured. We could take six in an ambulance. There were so many head injuries; it was horrible. They left home as strong young men. I thought to myself, this is worse than death."

— *Diane Silcox-Jarrett*

LIFE SAVERS War correspondent Ernie Pyle became attached to the 38th Evac and in his 1943 book, *Here Is Your War*, wrote of Margaret Pegram Mitchell *(above, left, at a Red Cross hospitality tent in England)* and her counterparts: "The nurses have already covered themselves with glory. The wounded have only praise for those who pulled them through. Our only deaths were those killed outright and those so badly wounded nothing could save them."

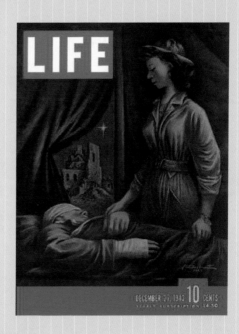

PATIENT CARE

Formed by a group of civilian doctors in Charlotte, the 38th Evacuation Hospital Unit was called to active duty on March 21, 1942. Its more than 600-member staff served in Africa and Italy.

Illustrator Fletcher Martin's portrait of 38th Evac nurse and First Lt. Martha Pegram Mitchell, which ran on the December 1943 cover of *Life* magazine *(above)*, brought attention to the courage of the Charlotte unit.

"When you are 22, you are eager to do things," said Mitchell. "I wanted to help with the war effort. Word got around Charlotte that the 38th Evac was looking for nurses, so I signed up. The hardest part was seeing the casualties. These were young men our age and they were coming to us after being hit with mortar shells. I remember one young man who had been hit so hard, he had abdominal wounds and his hip bones were shattered. He had so many holes we just had to put him back together. We had to collect blood from our unit in order to give him enough transfusions, but he made it."

— *Diane Silcox-Jarrett*

Remembering the Fallen

To Mothers of the Gold Star

His country called and he was gone,

That little boy of yours,

Who overnight became a man

And sailed for foreign shores;

No shadow marred his happiness

The day he said goodbye,

For valiantly you smiled to hide

The tear-drop in your eye.

Now Mother Earth holds to her breast

Secure from all alarms,

The one who only yesterday

You cradled in your arms;

And tho' the nation tenders you

Its gratitude untold,

Within your lonely window shines

A bright new star of gold.

— *Nellie Miles Paul,* The State: A Weekly Survey of North Carolina, *September 15, 1945*

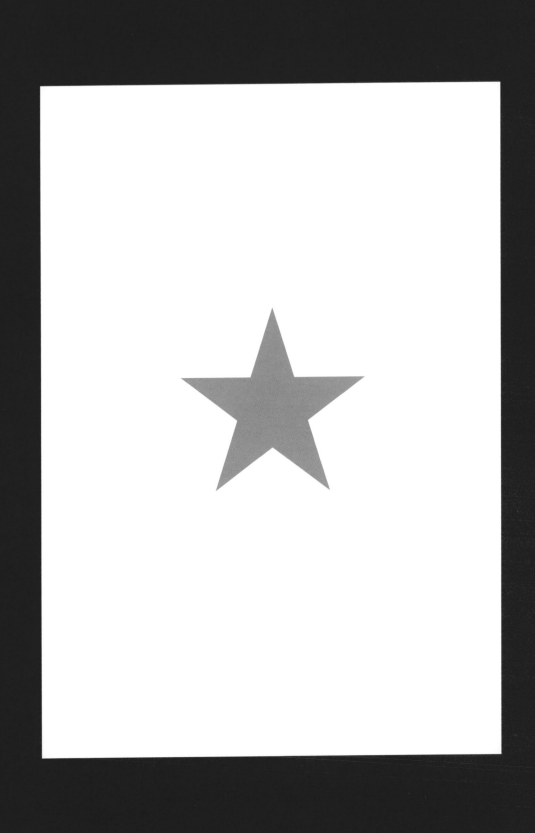

THE PREDDY BROTHERS

Combining eagle-eye vision, an aggressive nature, and nerves of steel, Maj. George Preddy established himself as an American ace in the European Theater.

He was a determined man. Rejected by the Navy three times because of his small size (5-feet-9, 120 pounds) and curved spine, Preddy joined the National Guard in 1940, then transferred to the U.S. Army Air Corps in 1941. Ultimately, the young airman from Greensboro joined the 34th Fighter Squadron, where his reputation as a fighter pilot quickly soared. He shot down his first German plane on December 1, 1943; three weeks later, he diverted enemy planes away from a disabled B-24 bomber. That feat earned him a Silver Star.

But it was his August 6, 1944, mission that brought Preddy his greatest fame. The pilot had stayed up into the wee hours of the morning, drinking and shooting craps, after being told bad weather had canceled plans for the day. Higher-ups, however, changed their minds.

"So 15 minutes after George finally turned in, they woke him up and said, 'You're leading a mission today,'" said Joe Noah, cousin and co-author of *George Preddy, Top Mustang Ace*. Preddy guzzled coffee and breathed oxygen to sober up. He not only led the mission but shot down six planes in the space of five minutes.

That fall, the 25-year-old took command of the 328th Fighter Squadron, which downed a record 24 enemy planes in a single mission. On Christmas Day, 1944 during a dog-fight over Belgium, Preddy's plane was hit by Allied fire.

His parents did not learn of his death until January 1945. Three months later, George's brother Bill, also a pilot, was killed during a mission over Czechoslovakia. They were buried side by side at the Lorraine American Military Cemetery in St. Avold, France.

— *Jimmy Tomlin*

PARALLEL LIVES George Preddy indicates the day's kills from his Cripes A'Mighty 3rd on July 18, 1944. Also an accomplished fighter pilot, George's brother, Lt. Bill Preddy, returns to England after a mission in July 1944. Nine months later, both brothers will be killed in action.

Jan. 23, 1945
Dearest Mother & Dad,
Yesterday I learned about George. …
What I have to say now is difficult to
explain because I hardly understand it
myself. There is no use to say not to
grieve, for I know that is impossible. It is
useless to say try and forget, for we can't
and shouldn't. We should remember, but
in doing so we should look at it in the
true light. A man's span on this earth is
not measured in years.

Above all, that is least important. To
find happiness, success, and most important, to find God is the Zenith of any
man's worldly activities. I think a man
has not lived until these things have been
achieved. … Yes, George knew a full, rich
life. He surely reached out and touched
the face of God many times. … I close
offering you my eternal love and devo-
tion. Let us carry on as George wanted
and may we arrive at his standard.
Always love, Bill

source: The Preddy Foundation:
http://www.preddy-foundation.org/bill_preddy_bio.htm

SIX ON SIX On August 6, 1944, George Preddy sets a record for most German planes downed by a single pilot during one mission, earning him the Distinguished Service Cross.

352ND FG ASSN PHOTOGRAPHY ARCHIVES VIA SAM SOX, JR., ARCHIVIST

James F. "Frank" Russell (*far right*) of the Army Air Forces had already served his time overseas and been given a stateside assignment. But when his younger brother Phil earned his wings, he volunteered for more missions so that they could fly together.

"They felt young and invincible and were raring to go," said their sister, Betty Russell Hurd. "And at that time, there were no rules saying brothers couldn't serve together."

The Asheville natives arrived in England in early 1944 as part of a 10-man B-24 *Liberator* crew with the 67th Squadron. Frank was co-pilot; Phil, navigator. Aware of the risks but upbeat, Phil wrote to a friend, "Perhaps it is unfair to our folks, but I honestly believe our own overall chances are better. I don't believe there are many new crews better than we are."

On Easter eve, April 8, 1944, the 67th Squadron lost 11 aircraft over Germany. One of them was the Russell brothers' bomber. "Our plane caught fire and went into a spin immediately," said gunner Archie Thomas, who managed to parachute from the spiraling aircraft seconds before it dashed into the ground. He was the sole survivor.

— *Jimmy Tomlin*

COURTESY OF BETTY RUSSELL HURD

THE PRICE BROTHERS

It was in Liege, Belgium, on December 23, 1944, that the Price brothers of Rutherford County set eyes on each other for the first time in three years. Falls Price (*above, right*) was sitting in a café when he saw Arthur on the sidewalk — they resembled each other so much, there could be no mistake. Arthur, now just out of his teens, had followed Falls into the Army after being drafted in June 1943, and both had wound up serving in Europe. On this day of serendipitous reunion, they talked endlessly, shared a meal, and had their photo taken before saying their goodbyes. Three days later, Arthur, a mine demolition expert, was killed by an exploding mine at the Rhine River.

source: *Real Heroes,* Anita Price Davis

THE SAVIOR OF MAYENNE

Two months after D-Day, the U.S. Army's 90th Infantry met up with the retreating Nazi army at the historic city of Mayenne some 130 miles from Paris. Two of the city's three bridges were already destroyed, and the Germans had wired the third one with explosives. Losing that bridge would have pinned the Americans in a punishing fight and left the ancient town in ruins.

Pvt. James D. McRacken of Red Springs was part of a small force of soldiers ordered to take the bridge. On August 5, 1944, the 28-year-old darted through 500 yards of machine-gun fire, crawling mortally wounded the last few feet. He reached the bridge and disarmed the bombs, then fell dead.

As the Americans routed the Germans, townspeople flocked to McRacken and covered his body with a shroud and dahlias. From that day forward, the North Carolinian became known as the "Savior of Mayenne." He was awarded several medals posthumously, including the Distinguished Service Cross. Charles De Gaulle placed a wreath on his grave at the American cemetery at Omaha Beach before the soldier's remains were returned to his hometown for burial.

Mayenne became an extended family to McRacken's widow, Mae, and daughter, Myrtis, who was a toddler when her father died. Through money raised as the result of a newspaper story about them in *The Charlotte Observer*, mother and daughter visited the French town in August 1961. There, they received Mayenne's heartfelt thanks and a painting of the bridge McRacken saved.

Following September 11, 2001, Mayenne residents gathered on the bridge in a show of support for their friends across the Atlantic.

CHAPTER FOUR

HOME FRONT

NORTH CAROLINA DURING WARTIME

"Roses are red. Violets are blue. Sugar is sweet. Remember?"
— *Walter Winchell, April 1942*

"Civilians can make a great contribution to the cause.
They can help to create and maintain a great morale."
— *North Carolina Gov. J. Melville Broughton, 1941*

HEAVY METAL In Raleigh, as around the state, North Carolinians worked to "scrap the Axis" through metal, rubber, and tin can drives.

7th WAR LOAN NOW-ALL TOGETHER

CAROLINA CAMPAIGNS
For the Cause

Not a single North Carolinian was unaffected by the war. Countless campaigns were implemented in support of what was happening overseas. From scrap drives to government rations, from war bonds to entertaining the troops to planting a garden, everyone pitched in. Make do with less became the rallying cry. Ration books came with instructions that said, "If you don't need it, don't buy it."

A STRONG DEFENSE Preparing for the worst, members of the Junior Red Cross of Cabarrus County teach first aid to classmates.

RATIONAL THINKING

I've covered the "ration front" for the past three years in a small Tar Heel town and I've found out the great truth of the statement that "if you want to sell anything, just ration it." I'm firmly convinced that rationing — because it is not liked by a liberty-loving public in this country — is the only thing in the world that will turn the "best" people into wartime violators of their country's regulations.

It all started, so far as I am concerned, when I learned one day that a farmer had reported to the Rationing Board that a hog on his farm had eaten up his gas book and he (the farmer) wanted a replacement.

It's been amazing, too, how many rationing books of all kinds apparently need to be washed. In one month's time at the Rationing Board in Wilson, 20 persons applied for replacements of various books they said were damaged when they were left in clothing sent to the laundry.

It's remarkable, also, how many rationing books in this nation get "lost in the mail." In Wilson in the last six months 200 'A' books for gas have been reported lost in the mail alone and not a single one of them has ever shown up as "found."

Sugar is another remarkable item on the rationing list. There are 50,000 persons in Wilson County. In normal times possibly 5,000 of them did actual canning with use of sugar. Last year over 20,000 persons applied for canning sugar in the Wilson Rationing Board.

— *John G. Thomas,*
The State: A Weekly Survey of North Carolina,
June 2, 1945

No. 802534 BI

WAR RATION BOOK No. 3

Void if altered

NOT VALID WITHOUT STAMP

Identification of person to whom issued: PRINT IN FULL

William F Parker

(First name)   (Middle name)   (Last name)

Street number or rural route 2015 Asheboro

City or post office Greensboro   State N. C.

AGE	SEX	WEIGHT	HEIGHT	OCCUPATION
46	Male	190 Lbs.	6 Ft. 1 In.	Mail Carrier

SIGNATURE William F Parker

(Person to whom book is issued. If such person is unable to sign because of age or incapacity, another may sign in his behalf.)

WARNING

This book is the property of the United States Government. It is unlawful to sell it to any other person, or to use it or permit anyone else to use it, except to obtain rationed goods in accordance with regulations of the Office of Price Administration. Any person who finds a lost War Ration Book must return it to the War Price and Rationing Board which issued it. Persons who violate rationing regulations are subject to $10,000 fine or imprisonment, or both.

OPA Form No. R-130

LOCAL BOARD ACTION

Issued by _____

(Local board number)   (Date)

Street address _____

City _____   State _____

(Signature of issuing officer)

RUBBER MEETS THE ROAD

According to Lew Powell's *On This Day in North Carolina*, Alice Broughton *(left)*, wife of the governor, contributed a heavy stair-case mat from the Executive Mansion to the rubber re-cycling effort in July 1942. The first service station she approached with the mat, however, wouldn't take it. A *Raleigh Times* reporter who accompanied Mrs. Broughton wrote, "So the rubber was placed back in the box and carted across the street. There the fellows seemed to know what it was all about and gladly accepted the rubber. Perhaps it is because of stations like the first that more rubber has not been turned in."

SEEDS OF SUCCESS

On February 9, 1942, Victory Garden Week in North Carolina was proclaimed with the slogan "Vegetables for Vitality Needed for Victory in the War." Other posters exhorted people to, "Plant a Victory Garden: Our Food is Fighting." Home and community gardens sprouted; Raleigh alone had 4,000 Victory Gardens. In Kannapolis, the YMCA plowed 200 acres into 300 separate plots, free for the planting, and at harvest time ran a canning facility. In Johnston County, stores were closed on Wednesday afternoons for people to go home and work in their gardens. Governor Broughton urged gardeners to plant a great variety of vegetables and grow enough extra to get through the winter. "With one or two exceptions, we can get all the vitamins we need for good health from the family garden," he said, "but we can't get them by just planting a row of beans and tomatoes in the spring and a row of turnips in the fall."

DIG IN

The time for setting that victory garden of yours is at hand. Last year, thousands of new gardens were set out in North Carolina. They proved of inestimable value in helping out the food situation in the state. It's an important part of the war effort.
— The State: A Weekly Survey of North Carolina, *April 1, 1944*

CANNERY ROW During the war years, North Carolinians canned 28 million quarts of food and dried 8 million pounds of fruits and vegetables.

BUY WAR BONDS

INVESTING IN VICTORY

War bond booths became permanent features at schools, in movie theaters, and in grocery stores. In all eight War Loan campaigns, North Carolinians exceeded their quotas as the government raised $85.7 billion to help pay for the war.

STAR APPEAL Hollywood celebs John Payne and Jane Wyman promote war bond sales in Burlington.

FLOWER POWER

A Guilford County woman wrote Gov. J.M. Broughton that she had plucked a magnolia blossom from a park in Raleigh some years ago, and asked the Governor what she could do to ease her conscience. "Buy a war bond," the Governor replied.

— The State: A Weekly Survey of North Carolina, *January 29, 1944*

HELP UNTIL IT HURTS

I thought that I had bought all the war bonds I could possibly buy during the current drive. Then I read Ernie Pyle's article about his walk along the beach in France after the Invasion and I changed my mind. In case you did not read this particular article, it was the one in which he told of the dead and wounded soldiers strewn the length of the beach. He told of the letters from home, the family photographs, the Bibles, the clothes, all the dearest keepsakes of our boys abandoned by them as they went down under enemy fire. First I had to cry a spell, but when I was done with my weeping my first thought was "What can I do to help?" The only answer I could get was buy more war bonds.

— *Carol Dare, "Merely a Woman's Opinion,"* The State: A Weekly Survey of North Carolina, *July 1, 1944*

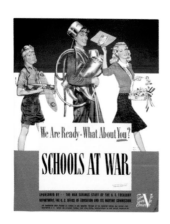

SCHOOL WORK

Children of all ages were encouraged to get involved in the war effort through the "Schools at War" program. At Long Grammar School in Concord, war bonds and stamps were available for purchase one day a week and a banner went to the classroom whose pupils bought the most. Special scrapbooks let students record their war activities. In his class' scrapbook at Edgemont School in Rocky Mount, fourth-grader Thurman Nail wrote, "We must save our shoes during this war. One way to take care of them is to keep them polished. When you get your shoes wet, you should not put them under the stove to dry because that dries the leather and makes it crack and wear out quicker." Near Fayetteville, first-graders at White Oak School wrote in verse about their gardening contribution. "We are planning a garden club. We will help our parents true. We will work to bring victory and feed our country too."

STAMP OF APPROVAL

In the fall of 1943 North Carolina schoolchildren bought 2,080 jeeps or an investment of $4,341,048.30. If 90 percent of the children in a school buy War Stamps regularly and take part in other "Schools at War" activities, the school is entitled to own and fly the United States Treasury Schools at War flag.

— The State: A Weekly Survey of North Carolina,
February 26, 1944

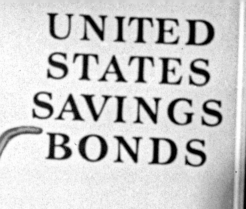

UNITED
STATES
SAVINGS
BONDS

ON SALE AT YOUR POST OFFICE OR BANK

JUNIOR ACHIEVEMENT A youngster at Bassett School in Rocky Mount invests his savings in the war effort.

LET US ENTERTAIN YOU

The United Service Organizations, better known as the USO, became synonymous with entertaining troops. According to Sarah McCulloh Lemmon, North Carolina had 103 USO clubs in 47 communities and 38 towns sponsored similar clubs. During the war, North Carolinians had donated $4 million to the USO and another $3 million to G.I. recreation programs operated by local governments. Separate USO clubs existed for white servicemen, black servicemen, and officers.

Staffed by volunteers, most of them women, and supported by local donations, the clubs became a home away from home, a place to write letters, read, watch movies, dance with local girls, and socialize. "Most of them just want to talk, talk about home, their girlfriends," said a USO Club hostess. "They didn't know what they were going to face." The first government-built USO club in the country opened in Fayetteville in November 1941.

USO Camp Shows brought movie stars and headliners to the troops, both stateside and overseas. In 1942, Betty Grable and Mickey Rooney made separate appearances at Fort Bragg. In 1944, boxing champion Joe Louis gave a three-round exhibition bout before a capacity crowd at the base.

— *David La Vere*

PATRIOTS ACT

When the United States entered World War II, patriotism surged on the North Carolina home front, with the ubiquitous fervor of the red, white and blue permeating every avenue of life. Love of and loyalty to country surfaced in expressions of appreciation, acts of kindness, and community solidarity as well as the occasional controversial — albeit powerful — reminder of the precious nature of dissent and tolerance.

A COMMUNITY OF FEW

Named around 1904 after a city in Japan, Oyama in Durham County immediately renamed itself after the Pearl Harbor attack. The community's newly adopted name was Few, after William Few, Duke University's first president.

LONE EAGLE

Agreeing with an angry citizen's opinion that Charles Lindbergh "does not deserve to have a street in Charlotte named for him," the city council voted in June 1941 to change the name of Lindbergh Drive to Avon Terrace. Many cities around the country took similar action in reaction to the famed aviator's opposition to the United States' increasing role in the war against Germany.

AC-CENT-TCHU-ATE THE POSITIVE Fort Bragg's dance band entertains guests at the Wilmington USO in 1944.

At Ease

Wartime sentiment infused North Carolina with a new creative energy. Songs about war, patriotism, loneliness, even Christmas filled our lives and set our feet to dancing — from the jitterbug to the fox trot. North Carolinians brought insight into the war in other ways, as well. Through art and literature, residents stateside were afforded bird's-eye views of the conflict — from the stark realities of the battlefields of France to the humorous world of military service.

And while the war made us give up Sunday drives and nylons, it didn't make us give up "The Lone Ranger," "The Shadow," or "Your Hit Parade." The golden age of radio brought Burns and Allen, Kate Smith, Bob Hope, and the Big Bands into wartime living rooms. It also brought the war. "We listened to the war news every night on WMFD in Wilmington," said Ese Baxley-Jarrett of Mount Gilead. "My parents wanted to know everything that was going on." The networks were so successful at that, soldiers in war zones joked that their families at home knew more about what was happening than they did.

BOOGIE WOOGIE BUGLE BOYS The big brass in the Cloudbusters, the first African-American band of the Navy Pre-Flight School, are "ablowin'" more than reveille in Chapel Hill.

VOICE OF A GENERATION

Edward R. Murrow's nightly eyewitness radio reports from the rooftops of London brought the German bombing of England into America's living rooms. "This … is London," he began.

Murrow was born a North Carolinian, son of a Quaker farming family outside of Greensboro. The CBS newsman's courage and integrity came from his upbringing, said brother Dewey Murrow. Their parents' intense religious and moral tutelage "branded us with their own consciences."

SEE HERE

Unlikely as it seemed at the time, being drafted into the Army in 1941 was the luckiest break budding writer Marion Hargrove could have hoped for. Sent to Fort Bragg for basic training, he busily turned his humorous misadventures into vignettes, which he sold to his old employer, *The Charlotte News*, for two dollars apiece. The next year, the articles were collected into a book, *See Here, Private Hargrove*. Just barely 23 years old, the North Carolina soldier became an overnight wartime literary sensation with the No.1 best-seller in the nation.

YOU CAN GO HOME AGAIN

See Here, Private Hargrove had its world premiere show this past week in Charlotte. Young Hargrove, now a sergeant and a veteran member of the staff of *Yank*, was catapulted to nationwide fame after his book became a best seller. Subsequently bought by Metro-Goldwyn-Mayer, it was developed into a picture. The producers announced the premiere would be held in the lanky youngster's hometown.

— The State: A Weekly Survey of North Carolina, *February 26, 1944*

THE HIT PARADE

1. "Boogie Woogie Bugle Boy"
2. "Chattanooga Choo Choo"
3. "Don't Sit Under the Apple Tree"
4. "I'll Be Home for Christmas"
5. "I'm Making Believe"
6. "Praise the Lord and Pass the Ammunition"
7. "Oh, What a Beautiful Mornin'"
8. "Sentimental Journey"
9. "White Christmas"
10. "The White Cliffs of Dover"

MUSIC IN THE AIR

The mood was so relaxed aboard a German submarine lurking off the North Carolina coast in early 1942 that the captain permitted swing music from Charlotte radio station WBT to be piped throughout the U-boat. In the galley, the chef banged pots in time with "Chattanooga Choo Choo."

AND THE OSCAR GOES TO

1941 – How Green was My Valley
1942 – Mrs. Miniver
1943 – Casablanca
1944 – Going My Way
1945 – The Lost Weekend

BLUE LAW BLUES

It was possible to see a movie on Sunday in 35 towns and cities across North Carolina in early 1941, but not in Charlotte. Life in the state's largest city was, in newspaperman W.J. Cash's words, "one continuous blue law." After the Army threatened to move its newly opened 2,000-man Charlotte Army Air Base, however, Charlotte City Council changed the law to allow Sunday movies and sporting events such as minor league baseball.

IN THE SWING Tommy Dorsey, Jo Stafford, and Frank Sinatra of the Pied Pipers – with Buddy Rich on the drums – livened UNC's gymnasium with the quintessential sound of Big Band.

MACMILLAN'S FRANCE

In addition to his regular duties as a soldier, Pvt. Henry Jay MacMillan of Wilmington painted his way through Normandy, Belgium, Holland, and Germany — whenever and wherever it was halfway safe to set up an easel. In notes accompanying his picture of G.I.s repairing a bridge at Maastricht in Holland, the unflappable artist remarked: "While painting this, I attracted many Dutch sightseers until a buzz bomb fell in the river. They then doffed their hats, bowed politely, and scurried for shelter."

THROUGH THE RUINS

We were going through the town of St. Lo (*left*), which was the most bombed-out, wrecked-up town you can imagine and in the middle of all the rubble, I looked over and said to my jeep driver, "I swear that fellow looks like he's painting over there." It turned out to be my friend Henry MacMillan from Wilmington, who had been assigned by his corps commander to just paint."

— *Army Capt. Dan Cameron, Normandy, 1944*

source: Special Collections, William Madison Randall Library, UNCW

TIL WE MEET AGAIN

Some heroes went off to battle while other heroes stayed home — working, rationing, raising children, coping with loneliness, and facing telegrams. But their thoughts were never far from one another.

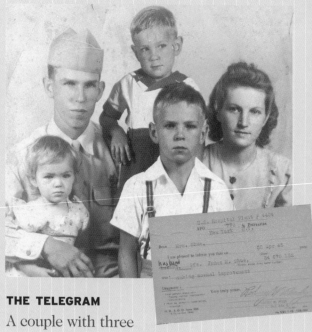

SEALED WITH A KISS

Norris Dearmon left his bride, Dorothy, crying at their front door in Kannapolis when he was drafted into the Army in December 1942 after just eight months of marriage. "She couldn't bear to take me down to the bus station. We were only 20 and had dated for four and a half years before we married. It was like we had always been together." Dorothy followed Norris to his posting in Denver and then to Maine, where he got his orders to Iceland. They wrote letters as a daily ritual while he was overseas. Dorothy signed hers with lipstick kisses and hand-drawn pictures of them squeezing hands. It was their special way of saying "I love you."

— *Diane Silcox-Jarrett*

THE TELEGRAM

A couple with three children, Celeste and James Shue were flabbergasted when he got his draft notice in 1944. "We had heard they were not taking men 27 years and older with children," said Celeste. "James was almost 28." He left his family in Landis and went to war.

Nearly a year later, Celeste was working at Linn-Corriher Mill when she saw a Western Union messenger walking toward her. "I was shaking all over." The telegram said James had been wounded in action, but nothing more.

A week later, a second telegram arrived, just as frightening. "It said he was doing as well as could be expected. I thought, what does that mean?" A third telegram told her his condition was improving, and then came a letter from James himself explaining he was in Germany and had been hit by shrapnel. After that she received a telegram saying he had returned to active duty. James returned to his family in 1946.

— *Diane Silcox-Jarrett*

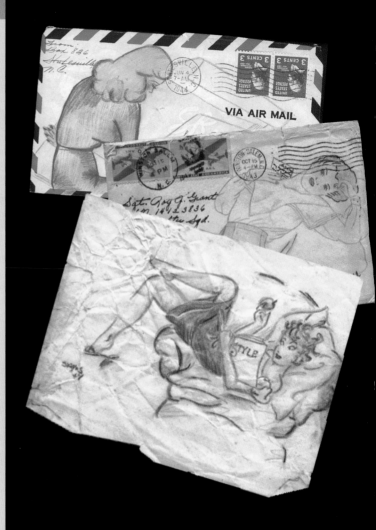

OH, TANNENBAUM

Into the bleakness of a German prisoner-of-war camp in December, Stanley Yelverton of Eureka helped bring an unexpected touch of Christmas warmth in 1944. A captive since the Battle of the Bulge weeks earlier, the young soldier found himself on a wood-cutting detail in the forest on Christmas Eve. Along with the firewood, he cut a small evergreen — and with great creativity and delight, the POWs soon turned it into a Christmas tree. "They took the paper from their cigarettes and crushed them up in balls to make ornaments to hang on the branches," said Al Yelverton, recounting the treasured story told to him by his dad. "I always told him, 'Now that was a North Carolina tree.'"

— *Diane Silcox-Jarrett*

MAIL CALL

Letters from home were popular with all troops, but the mail Sgt. Roy Jack Grant of Statesville received from his fiancé, Calveen Sherrill, ensured his popularity in the barracks. Stationed with the 351st Fighter Squadron off the North Sea coast, Grant and his fellow G.I.s looked forward to the colorful, sexy artwork she sent regularly. But the upside-down stamp was for Jack's eyes only — it was code for "I love you."

HOPE SPRINGS ETERNAL

"My happiest two days of World War II was when I covered Bob Hope's USO show on the island of New Caledonia in the South Pacific. In this photo Hope is introducing dancer Patty Thomas to the troops, receiving a riotous applause when he said, 'Men, this is what you are fighting for.' "

— *Hugh Morton, Grandfather Mountain, U.S. Army*

THE SPLENDID SPLINTER

Already acknowledged as one of the greatest hitters in the history of baseball, Ted Williams gamely continued to swing his bat while in Navy pre-flight training at UNC. Coming off a "Triple Crown" season with the Red Sox — leading the American League in home runs, batting average, and runs batted in — Williams stepped up to the plate in 1943 with his new team, the Chapel Hill Cloudbusters, in exhibition games to raise money for the war.

Williams was soon off to Indiana for the next phase of his training, but North Carolina forever stuck in his mind. "I'll never forget getting off the train at Chapel Hill just at dusk and marching up in front of the administration building with the other recruits," he said. "The cadets already there were hanging out the window watching us and as we passed, one guy hollered, 'Okay, Williams, we know you're there and you're going to be sorry.' " The indomitable baseball hero took it all in stride, saying later that "even the hairiest times were interesting."

— *Jimmy Tomlin*

ROSES ON TOBACCO ROAD

Faced with cancellation due to West Coast security fears after Pearl Harbor, the Rose Bowl Game found a one-time-only home in Durham on New Year's Day in 1942.

The cold, drizzly weather was a far cry from sunny California, but 56,000 fans flocked to Duke Stadium to see the displaced gridiron classic, filling extra bleachers hastily borrowed from UNC and N.C. State. The game between Oregon State and previously undefeated Duke was one of the most exciting in Rose Bowl history, though sadly ending in a 20–16 loss for the Blue Devils.

"Winning in Durham was special," said Martin Chaves, the triumphant Oregon State team captain. "Someone wins it in Pasadena every year."

Soon, the war supplanted football for the student athletes and their coaches. Wallace Wade, the Duke coach, was called up to serve in the Army and saw duty in Europe. Most of the players who suited up for the Rose Bowl would later serve in the war. Four of them — three from Duke, one from Oregon State — were reported killed in action.

— *Jimmy Tomlin*

TOO MANY BOWL GAMES

We are of the opinion that these "bowl games" in football are being overdone. When the folks out in California decided that a game between two outstanding teams would be a good feature in connection with their Tournament of Roses, they unquestionably had an excellent idea. …

The Rose Bowl game is, of course, primarily a commercial proposition. But it also carries with it a large element of sport. The other bowl games are entirely commercial. They don't decide anything and there is little excuse for their existence.

— The State: A Weekly Survey
of North Carolina,
January 4, 1941

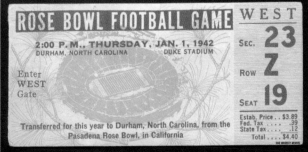

ROSE BOWL FOOTBALL GAME

WEST

2:00 P.M., THURSDAY, JAN. 1, 1942
DURHAM, NORTH CAROLINA   DUKE STADIUM

Enter
WEST
Gate

Transferred for this year to Durham, North Carolina, from the
Pasadena Rose Bowl, in California

SEC. **23**

ROW **Z**

SEAT **19**

Estab. Price . . $3.89
Fed. Tax 39
State Tax 12
Total . . . $4.40

by these North Carolina girls tell you

Come on in—the WAVES are Fine!

...important services—the WAVES of the United States Navy.

TRAVEL Anne Tisdale of Rocky Mount had always dreamed of travel to far, interesting places. "Now I'm actually here in New York," she says, "and I'm looking forward to seeing many other interesting places during my Naval service." You will, too—when you're a WAVE of the United States Navy!

EXCITEMENT Dull, commonplace work couldn't satisfy Pape White of Gastonia. She wanted an important, exciting job. "I'm training for it now," she writes. "I want to operate a Link Trainer—teaching 'blind flying.' It's exciting work and I wouldn't trade for any other job in the world! Nor would you!"

SMARTNESS Like every girl, Mc Guillery (left) of Asheville loves pretty clothes. She's with them in the WAVES! "Every one uniforms was designed by Mainbocher and you know what that means in fashion!" she says. "No wonder every style...

Help WIND-U Bus

...wish has been fulfilled. Won by years of deadly struggle. With d's help, we have prevailed. Now we have a chance to make other wish come true. For most in, the outlook is a bright one. we will simply use the brains, the the energy, the enterprise... materials and resources... with ...rch we won our war, we can't fail

to win the peace and to make this true by buying bonds today... buying them regularly... and holding on to them in spite of all temptation.

There's no safer, surer investment in the world. You can count on getting back $4 for every $3 you put in —as surely as you can count on being a day older tomorrow.

So why not be patriotic and smart at the same time!

Your wishes have been wrapped in that bright outlook. Your wish for a cottage by a lake. For your boy's college education. For a trip you long to take. For a "cushion" against emergencies and unforeseen needs.

You can make these wishes come...

FULFILL YOUR WISH—BUY EXTRA BONDS
IN THE GREAT **VICTORY LO**...

...LON SUPPLY COMPANY   THE ST...

"Corners are turned like _so_, Mrs. Newlywed!"

...EN HE COMES ...ME AND YELLS HELLO, MOM!"

Ma...
Occ...
Yo...

**ELE...
DI...**

As if you needed an **occasion** to buy these marvelous new electric ranges! Bu...... we all need a little stimulus to do some of th... things we know we should. So why not g... that range you've been yearning for, **now**, a... celebrate his homecoming with meals that o... do anything you've ever cooked?

Current range models are more efficient, m... flexible, more beautiful than ever! See ... in the appliance department of your fav... store today.

Play dumb, and let him show off his G. I. bed-making skill. In handling your Fieldcrest Sheets, he'll admire their smoothness and whiteness, and he'll bow to you for your good ju...... in choosing them. DURACALE, long-wearing per...... ...GATE, heavy muslin; WEARWELL, muslin... ...stores you'll find these Field...... ...ta and Bed-spre...

MA...

Fieldcrest
SHEETS
ALWAYS DISTINCTIVE   ALWAYS DEPENDABLE
...tion · Spray, N. C.

Duke POWER COMP...

VICTORY
BUY
UNITED
STATES
WAR
BONDS
AND
STAMPS

GASTONIA
Combed YARN
CORPORATIO
Gastonia, North Carolin...

Power for Defense!

In North Carolina's Most Active Defense Area

★ **CAMP DAVIS**
★ **FORT FISHER**
★ **North Carolina Shipbuilding Co.**

In addition to supplying Electric Power for these vital defense projects, Tide Water Power Company is supplying electric service to approximately 25,000 customers in this fast growing coastal area.

We are proud to have a part in providing the essential requisites for National Defense.

TIDE WATER POWER COM...

Let's STOP WASTE— *And Help Stop Hitler!*

WASTE Helps Hitler! Yo... frigerator is a food saf...

CHAPTER FIVE

VICTORY

A NEW ROAD HOME

"It will be a great day for me and other North Carolinians out here
when we get the word that we are going to head for home.
I'll be satisfied to remain in North Carolina for the rest of my life,
and I'll be willing to leave it up to others to travel around the world.
I have found no better place than my native state."

— Sgt. L.M. Wilkerson of Gastonia writing to
The State: A Weekly Survey of North Carolina, April 21, 1945

WAR ENDS

HAPPY DAYS ARE HERE AGAIN
Celebrations erupt on Greensboro's Elm Street after Japanese Emperor Hirohito announces an unconditional surrender on August 14, 1945. To make sure the long-awaited celebration doesn't get out of hand, Gov. Gregg Cherry suspends the sale of alcoholic beverages for the day.

NATIONAL ARCHIVES

THE END
Unconditional Surrender

Eight days after Adolf Hitler committed suicide in bomb-ravaged Berlin, the Third Reich collapsed. With Germany's official surrender on May 7, 1945, the Allied strategy of "Europe First" had succeeded but at an enormous cost; the caprice of war had shattered Europe. With the news three months later that Japan had surrendered following atomic assaults on Hiroshima and Nagasaki, North Carolinians were relieved that the war had finally ended. More than 4,000 Tar Heels lost their lives; many of those who had survived were physically and emotionally battered. The harrowing news of the Holocaust further shocked the state. But the defeat of the Axis powers meant several hundred thousand North Carolina soldiers and sailors would be returning home — a home strikingly different from the one they left.

MARCH TO BERLIN The 78th Infantry Division from Camp Butner raises the American flag over the beautiful German hamlet of Spangenberg near the Rhine River in the spring of 1945.

"Harry, the President is dead."

— Eleanor Roosevelt to Harry S. Truman, April 12, 1945

THE ASHEVILLE CITIZEN — CITY EDITION

HARRY S. TRUMAN TAKES OATH OF PRESIDENT AS FRANKLIN D. ROOSEVELT DIES OF STROKE; WORLD SECURITY PROGRAM WILL BE CONTINUED

THE DEATH OF THE PEOPLE'S PRESIDENT

When Franklin Roosevelt died on the 83rd day of his fourth term, the nation and the world keenly felt the loss. Britain's Winston Churchill broke down while relaying the news to the House of Commons. Vice President Truman said, "I felt like the moon, the stars, and all the planets have fallen on me." Eleanor Roosevelt had personally broken the news to him at the White House before departing for Georgia. Truman asked her, "Is there anything we can do for you?" She replied, "Tell us what we can do. You're the one in trouble now."

Recognizing that many considered Roosevelt indispensable to winning the war, President Truman said in his first official pronouncement, "You may be sure that we will prosecute the war on both fronts, East and West, with all the vigor we possess, to a successful conclusion."

NEWS & RECORD

THE LONG WAY HOME

When news of President Roosevelt's demise at his Warm Springs, Georgia, retreat reached Fort Benning the afternoon of April 12, the head of the post's intelligence and security unit pulled Bob Rankin *(front row, left)* aside. "Sort of casually he said, 'Sergeant, would you like to go to Warm Springs?' And I said, 'Yes, sir, I really would.'" The 27-year-old soldier from High Point, son of a casket-maker, did not learn until the next morning he had been chosen for an elite military squad that would escort the president's body to the Georgia train station for the long trip home to his Hyde Park estate in New York. Before departing, Mrs. Roosevelt "went to each one of us and shook our hands. That impressed me. She was a wonderful and gracious lady."

MIDNIGHT TRAIN FROM GEORGIA From Georgia and through the Carolinas, Virginia, and finally into Washington, large crowds gathered to watch Roosevelt's funeral train pass. A hushed crowd of about 10,000 men, women, and children, their heads bared, met the train when it arrived in Greensboro at 12:47 a.m. that Saturday. Only the sound of "Taps" being played broke the silence.

THE BANALITY OF EVIL

"There surged around me an evil-smelling stink, men and boys reached out to touch me. They were in rags and the remnants of uniforms. Death already had marked many of them, but they were smiling with their eyes. ... I pray you to believe what I have said about Buchenwald. I reported what I saw and heard, but only part of it. For most of it, I have no words."

— *Edward R. Murrow at Buchenwald concentration camp* (below), *Germany, "They Died 900 a Day in 'the Best' Nazi Death Camp," CBS, April 16, 1945*

ALL IMAGES: NATIONAL ARCHIVES

RESCUE AND LIBERATION

"You were to be careful not to overfeed any prisoners as they had not adjusted to their shrunken stomachs and they would have to adjust gradually to a normal diet. We were allowed to give them a bit of chocolate, a spoonful of food and that was all that we were supposed to give them at one time."

— *Aaron May, Southport, with the U.S. Army at Dachau concentration camp, Germany*

source: Special Collections,
William Madison Randall Library, UNCW

Tobacco Sales
Up 27 Per Cent

WINSTON-SALEM JOURNAL

BIG 3 SLATED TO PROCLAIM VICTORY IN EUROPE TODAY

Hannegan Nomination Is Confirmed After Attack

World Conference Success Assured, Molotoff Asserts

AP Discloses Exclusively That Nazis Surrendered

Unconditional German Surrender Is Reported Signed but War Rages On in Czechoslovakia

Allies Use Airfield On Tarakan

Mt. Airy Men Fined For OPA Violations

Belgian King, Queen Freed

Yanks Root Out Japs On Okinawa

U.S. Officers In Prague; Breslau Falls

Truman Will Go on Air At 9 A.M.

TWO DOWN AND ONE TO GO

Germany capitulated last week. Our people took the news more or less in their stride. There was comparatively little carousing due to the fact that we knew the job we are working on hasn't been finished. From one end of the nation to the other, however, there was a feeling of thanksgiving that another of our enemies had surrendered and that the great struggle had now narrowed down to the last one.

— The State:
A Weekly Survey of North Carolina,
May 12, 1945

VIVA LA FRANCE French citizens express their gratitude to American soldiers following the country's liberation.

GROUND ZERO

At precisely 8:15:17 a.m. on August 6, 1945, Maj. Thomas Ferebee *(right in photo)* of Mocksville, bombardier aboard the B-29 *Enola Gay*, pushed a lever and watched a 9,000-pound bomb fall toward Hiroshima. The pilot, Col. Paul Tibbetts, had hand-picked Ferebee for his crew, calling him the "best bombardier who ever looked through the eyepiece of a Norden bombsight." Forty-three seconds after Ferebee yelled "Bomb away!" the sky erupted in dazzling light, and the aircraft veered sharply away to safety.

Ferebee, a star athlete at Lees-McRae College in Banner Elk, had flirted with the idea of playing professional baseball before he joined the Army Air Forces in 1940. At the age of 26, he had completed more than 60 missions in Europe and North Africa.

The project Tibbetts tapped him for was so secret even the crew didn't know they were carrying an atomic bomb until the plane was en route to Japan.

Three days after the bombing of Hiroshima, a different B-29 crew dropped one on Nagasaki. Five days later, the Japanese government surrendered. Ferebee's brother Bill was serving with the Navy in the Pacific when he learned of Tom's part in ending the war. "I heard a lot of men tell Tom he probably saved their lives. I was in the Philippines and was headed to Japan, so he might've saved my life, too."

— *Jimmy Tomlin*

SURRENDER OF JAPANESE MADE OFFICIAL

Liberated Physicians Say Thousands Died in Camps

PRESIDENT HAILS BIRTH OF AN ERA OF WORLD PEACE

Capitulation Document Signed Aboard Missouri in Tokyo Bay

UNSETTLING VICTORY

"I was on a ship at Guam when we heard that Hiroshima had been bombed. There was, of course, relief that the war might be over and we wouldn't have to stay there any longer. But there was a kind of hush and a sense of terror that pervaded the whole ship. People just knew that we had entered a new world, and I was really proud of my shipmates that they didn't rejoice and said, 'Good for them.' That was too horrible a thing for anybody to take pleasure in."

— *Walter Harrelson of Bolivia, N.C.,*
with the U.S. Navy in the Pacific

source: Special Collections,
William Madison Randall Library, UNCW

LAST ACT

George Rogers of Whiteville, a communications officer with the Navy, was aboard the USS *Missouri (left)* during the formal Japanese surrender ceremony on September 2, 1945. "When we sailed into Japanese waters, it was a very odd feeling to be anchored out in the sea and have lights on the ship that first night because we didn't know exactly what to expect, whether there would be any more planes coming off the island or not. But there wasn't any trouble. When we went into Tokyo Bay, you could see the Japanese riding bicycles on the shoreline. That was a strange feeling. A group of us went up to Tokyo and saw the different sights. There wasn't much left. You wondered how they did as much as they did."

source: Special Collections,
William Madison Randall Library, UNCW

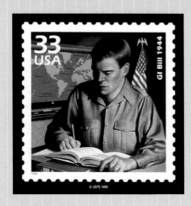

HOMEWARD BOUND

The thoughts of people everywhere was to get on with their lives. With peacetime came an end to rationing and the production of automobiles, washing machines, refrigerators, and television sets. The postwar Baby Boom brought 2 million new North Carolinians into the world.

BACK TO SCHOOL

Called by its beneficiaries "the greatest thing to come out of World War II," the 1944 G.I. Bill made it possible for millions of veterans to buy their own homes, learn a trade, start businesses, and further their education. Trailer parks and Quonset huts sprang up at North Carolina State in Raleigh to accommodate the unprecedented deluge. Some of Duke University's influx of students lived at Camp Butner and commuted to class. At Chapel Hill, facilities built for the Navy's Pre-Flight School provided extra accommodations. The Woman's College at Greensboro, after rescinding its prohibition against married students during the war, had 54 veterans among its student body by 1946.

G.I. TOWN

The 150 homes were modest, just four little rooms, and they initially had no fully equipped bathrooms, but the prefabricated-housing community that Charles Cannon created on Cannon Mills property in Kannapolis *(left)* was met with a sigh of relief by veterans returning to civilian life and eager to get their own place. Tenants paid $10 a month rent, which included water service and garbage collection. G.I. Town's paved streets, sidewalks, and trees became home to hundreds of mill families. "It was a nice life," remembered Ethel Wise. "There were children running everywhere, and we knew they were safe."

HARLEM RENAISSANCE

The G.I. Bill enabled soldier Romare Bearden, born in Charlotte and later acclaimed as one of the pre-eminent artists of his generation, to study at the Sorbonne in Paris. *(Pictured above: Bearden's* Carolina Shout.*)*

NOTHING COULD BE FINER

The *North Carolina* returned to the United States on October 17, 1945 — though not home to the state for which she was named. First moored at Boston, the ship moved into "mothballs" in New Jersey two years later. Technologically obsolete, the grand vessel sat until 1958, when the government announced plans to scrap her. Turn the *North Carolina* into scrap? Those were fighting words in North Carolina — sparking the beginning of a rescue of epic proportions.

James S. Craig Jr. of Wilmington championed the idea of buying the *North Carolina* and turning her into a floating memorial. Soon the entire state rallied to bring her home. In 1961, Gov. Terry Sanford created the *North Carolina* Battleship Commission to "acquire, transport, berth, equip, maintain, and exhibit the ship as a permanent memorial." He appointed Hugh Morton as its chair.

To fund the memorial, Morton created a "Save Our Ship" campaign. Anyone donating $100 or raising $500 would be officially commissioned an "admiral" of the "North Carolina Navy." Anyone donating $5 would receive free admission. To involve children, when every student in a school gave 10 cents, the entire student body received a special admission price. More than 700,000 schoolchildren contributed to the cause. In fact, one-quarter of the $345,000 raised came from schools; many of them reported 100 percent participation.

On October 2, 1961, crowds lined the banks of the Cape Fear River to watch an armada of tugboats push the ship up the river to the Wilmington waterfront. The *North Carolina* was finally home.

— *David La Vere*

HOME SWEET HOME The *North Carolina* fought in nearly 50 engagements in the Pacific. In the eastern Solomon Islands near Australia in 1942, her big guns were being fired so furiously that a sister ship radioed in alarm, "Are you on fire?"

Today, resting on the Cape Fear, the *North Carolina* is one of the state's most popular attractions, offering exhibits, special performances, and events that illuminate the extraordinary history of the ship and honor the memory of the state's veterans who died in the war.

CHAPTER SIX

REMEMBRANCE

NORTH CAROLINA'S "FINEST HOUR"

"No North Carolina city, no town, no rural section escaped
the loss of life during World War II. These are the men to
whom our State ... should never fail to pay tribute."

— *U.S. Secretary of War and Goldsboro native Kenneth Royall*

60 YEARS LATER

Honoring a Generation

Year by year, World War II grows ever dimmer in America's collective living memory. It is a sad reality that on a typical day in North Carolina, we say goodbye to another 40 men and women who served their country during the war. It's a reality that impels us to cherish and preserve the memories of a generation as well as honor those who are now gone. As Americans and North Carolinians, we would do well to say the words these heroes have probably never heard often enough. "Thank you."

GIVING THANKS On the grounds of the state capitol, the North Carolina Veterans' Memorial honors the men and women who served in World War I, World War II, and the Korean War.

A SOLDIER'S GOODBYE
ED HEATH

On a hot afternoon in June 2004, a few dozen mourners came to pay their respects to James Edwin "Ed" Heath, 83, a native of High Point who was being laid to rest with full military honors.

An American flag cloaked the coffin. Guns boomed a salute. A bugler sounded "Taps." Two members of the Randolph County Honor Guard folded the flag into a neat, precise triangle and placed it in the hands of Ed Heath's widow Betty. "Ma'am," one of the two veterans said softly, "on behalf of a grateful nation, we present to you this flag as a token of appreciation for the honorable and faithful service rendered by your loved one."

Infantry, he fought in the Battle of the Bulge and other major battles and came home with five Bronze Stars. Lawrence wants a burial like Heath's when his time comes.

By the traditional definition, Ed Heath was not a war hero. He was simply a young man, then a student at High Point College, who agreed to put his life on hold and do whatever his country needed of him. He enlisted in the Army Air Forces in 1942 and became a sergeant in the 57th Bomb Wing stationed in Corsica, Italy, and North Africa. His job was to schedule bombing runs, and he scheduled countless numbers of them.

❝I think it's our duty to give a military funeral for any veteran who wants it, because they've earned it.❞

The men of the honor guard did not know Ed Heath, but they understood the sacrifices he had made. "I think it's our duty to give a military funeral for any veteran who wants it, because they've earned it," said Wade Lawrence, of Asheboro, himself a decorated veteran of the war. He was just 20 years old when his outfit waded ashore at Omaha Beach in Normandy a few days after D-Day. A sergeant in Patton's 3rd

When the war ended, Ed Heath returned to High Point and resumed his life. He never talked much about his experience. He was a stickler about flying the flag on patriotic holidays. "Dad was proud of serving his country," said daughter LuAnne Heath Tywater. "He felt like it was a necessary thing to do to ensure better times going forward. I think most veterans, like my father, felt it was their duty."

— *Jimmy Tomlin*

FULL MILITARY HONORS Members of the Randolph County Honor Guard fold the American flag draped over Ed Heath's coffin to present it to his widow.

EXPRESSIONS OF GRATITUDE
EDDIE HART

For nearly 60 years, Betty Habets-Vrancken and her brother Johan have proudly tended the grave of Pvt. Eddie Hart, a young farmer from the Lenoir County town of LaGrange they never knew.

Killed in action on April 12, 1945, Hart was buried at the Netherlands American Cemetery near Betty and Johan's hometown. The 60-acre cemetery was a gift to the United States from the Dutch people in appreciation for the liberation of their country. The Dutch also established an adoption program, which included caring for the more than 18,000 graves and writing to the soldiers' families back home.

Betty was 22 years old in 1946 when she adopted the grave of Private Hart, vowing to visit and bring flowers regularly. She wrote to his sister Hattie in Lenoir County: "Dear Miss Hart, I am a Dutch girl and I live in the south part of Holland. I guess you know that there is buried your older brother Eddie and I have adopted his grave. I hope, dear Miss Hart, that this will be a little better for you to know that your brother's grave is not lonely and forgotten."

In the 1950s, Betty moved to the United States, but her brother stayed behind and continued as caretaker. After meeting Betty Habets-Vrancken in 2000, Brenda Hughes of Wrightsville Beach produced a documentary she titled *Thank You, Eddie Hart* to honor the memory of those who served and died. Hughes said that her 60-minute film, which premiered in 2004 on public television stations, "demonstrates that ordinary people can do most extraordinary things."

> **"I hope, dear Miss Hart, that this will be a little better for you to know that your brother's grave is not lonely and forgotten."**

CARROLL T. WOOD

It was 1987 when Ira David Wood III arrived at the Normandy American Cemetery in Collevile-sur-Mer, France, walked the endless rows of white markers, and finally stood before Plot C, Row 28, Grave 29. It was the grave of his uncle Carroll, of Halifax County, a first lieutenant in the 79th Infantry Division who fell in combat and died August 1, 1944.

David Wood's father, also with the Army in France, did not learn of Carroll's death for weeks, though the brothers were just miles away from one another at the time. Upon hearing the devastating news, he went into his tent and wept for three days.

Years passed. The family knew Carroll was buried in Normandy but did not know the name of the cemetery. In the meantime, David Wood had grown up and become an actor — a sensation, in fact, with his enormously popular adaptation of *A Christmas Carol*. The musical comedy premiered in Raleigh in 1974 and has been performed there every year since. It has also enjoyed success on tour. One of those tours was to Compiegne, France.

On a visit to Compiegne to see the theater several months in advance of the show, David Wood intended to use his spare time to search for his uncle's cemetery. But there turned out to be no spare time, as he lamented to a new acquaintance at a party. She at once became teary-eyed and took his hands in hers. "You must go," she cried. "He came to save us, and he died alone."

The next day, a man who had been at the party presented Wood with an index card. On it was the precise location of Carroll Wood's grave. He explained that his father had been a member of the French Underground during the war. Together, they had found the information.

Wood rented a car and drove to the cemetery. Historic and beautiful, overlooking Omaha Beach, it is the resting place of 9,386 Americans. "I was immediately struck by the fact that the number of graves was almost double the population of Enfield, where I was raised. I realized, too, that each cross or Star of David represented an entire grieving family — mother, father, wife, brothers, sisters. As I tried to multiply that feeling of loss by the number of graves, it became emotionally overwhelming." He spent nearly three hours there. "I never knew him — but I feel, in some special way, that I know him now."

Months later, David Wood returned to Compiegne to perform *A Christmas Carol*. His sister, Carol Wood — named for their uncle — sat in the audience. By now, Wood understood the poignancy of his performing in Compiegne, having learned that, had his uncle lived, this is where the movement of troops would have brought him.

As he stood on stage, just before the show's closing musical number, he said quietly, "This is for Lt. Carroll T. Wood," and began to sing "The First Noel."

It was, he said later, "as though an incomplete cycle had finally been completed."

— *Jimmy Tomlin*

A FATHER'S LOVE
PETE LYNN

On the night of November 4, 1944, Ruth Lynn awoke to the familiar sound of her husband, Pvt. Felmer Llonza "Pete" Lynn, whistling as he walked home from his job at a nearby cotton mill in the small town of Kings Mountain. She knew it couldn't be him — Pete was in Germany — but she got out of bed and went to the door anyway, just to be sure. Nobody. She sat on the front porch for the rest of the night, fearful the whistling was a bad omen. In her diary she wrote, "Afraid something happened to our daddy."

Four months later, a telegram proved her right. Pete had been killed, most likely on November 4 or 5. "Got telegram Wednesday about 4:30," Ruth wrote in her diary. "Can't believe it."

At the time, Ruth had two daughters under the age of five and was seven months pregnant with another. When the third daughter arrived on May 6, 1945, Ruth named her Felma Ruth, but called her Petie.

Petie Lynn Bass remembers the pain of growing up without a father and still hungers to know him. "My mother would try to tell me about him and what he was like. As a little girl, I remember thinking that maybe one day I'd actually see him. After all these years, it still bothers me."

Petie knows him only through her mother's stories and an array of mementos: a billfold engraved with his name, the New Testament he carried overseas, his Purple Heart, newspaper clippings from the *Kings Mountain Herald* reporting his death, the gold star Ruth hung in the front window of their home.

She also has her mother's diary and a bundle of letters the couple exchanged. The diary portrays a despondent woman, with entries such as "There seems no reason to go on." The letters, by contrast, depict a husband and wife who were mad about each other and about their family. "That's really about all he talks about," said Petie, "how much he misses her, how much he misses the two girls, how he can't wait to come home. From his letters, I can tell he was totally devoted to his girls."

Pete's body arrived home on November 14, 1947, Ruth having successfully battled to have his body exhumed from a military cemetery in Belgium and brought back to Kings Mountain. Little Petie was two years old when they laid her father to rest at Mountain Rest Cemetery.

Petie said she understands why her parents' generation is referred to as "the greatest generation." "So much was required of them. First they went through the Depression, and then World War II. Their lives were put on hold. Think of all those widows and their children who had to pick up and move on. I've never known anyone with the strength that they had."

— *Jimmy Tomlin*

DOC LONG

I went back to France in September 2004 on the occasion of the 60th anniversary of that country's liberation. Like many thousands of other American G.I.s, I had fought there during the war.

My daughter, son-in-law, and I were there on a tour with the Lorraine Battle Memorial Association, along with a group of French historians of World War II who also served as our guides.

" Over and over, the people we met told us how indebted they were to Americans. 'You made sacrifices so we could be free again, they said.' "

The tour took us to towns, villages, and battlefields where I had seen combat with a rifle company in the 79th Infantry. What we saw now in those places was celebration upon celebration.

The celebrations had been in full swing since June 6 — which will be remembered forever in history as the date Allied troops landed on the shores of Normandy and began the liberation of Europe.

In towns and villages, we saw pictures of American G.I.s, nurses, and Red Cross volunteers that had been made into banners and put on lampposts. Store windows and buildings also displayed signs in recognition of the American liberators.

We attended some 21 different celebrations. Most were attended by French army personnel, town officials, and local citizens. Bands played both our national anthem and theirs, and also "Taps."

At one village, a throng of little children had lined up to welcome us. Each held up a large placard printed with a word. Strung together, the words made a sentence that read in English, "We the children of Sanlang welcome the American Veterans and thank them for what they did for our country!" A microphone was handed to the children and, in turn, they repeated the words they were holding. This was one of the most touching moments of our trip, a testimonial that the French continue to teach each succeeding generation about the history our two countries share.

At another event, we met a frail, 93-year-old gentleman who had made a special effort to be there to personally thank American veterans. With a friend interpreting, he told of witnessing his brother's execution at the hands of the Nazis. If it had not been for the American soldiers, he and the rest of his family would not have survived.

A lady told us her story of being wounded in the war as an innocent bystander, only 11 years old. Shrapnel had struck her in the forehead, taking out one of her eyes. As she lay injured and abandoned, an American medic scooped her up and took her to a hospital. He saved her life, she said.

Over and over again, the people we met told us how indebted they were. "You made sacrifices so we could be free again," they said. They knew on a personal level that the young men who died on their soil were sons, brothers, uncles, husbands, and fathers. They vowed they would never forget — that they could never forget.

— *William Henry "Doc" Long*
(pictured far left)

ACKNOWLEDGMENTS

The stories and photographs on the preceding pages could not have come together as a book without the generosity and efforts of many people. Writers David La Vere, Diane Silcox-Jarrett, and Jimmy Tomlin provided the book's backbone. Copy editors Betty Work and Amanda Hiatt worked tirelessly researching, fact checking, and proofreading. Our State staff members Cheryl Bissett, Elizabeth Hudson, Claudia Royston, Debbie West, Amy Jo Wood, and Bets Woodard proved invaluable with their perspectives on the book's concept, design, and direction. Photographer Mark Wagoner and studio manager Jill Davis employed their superior skills photographing memorabilia from the 1940s. Frances and Will Best, Lyda Adams Carpén, Bobbie Cook, James Ellington, Cheminne Taylor-Smith, Walter Turner, all offered insightful ideas and suggestions.

Others around the state and the Southeast helped keep this project on course. An enormous debt is owed to Stephen E. Massengill, iconographic archivist at the North Carolina Office of Archives and History, for his help in gathering photographs. Military Collections Archivist Si Harrington, also a member of the Archives and History staff, led us to many of the veterans we profiled. At UNC Chapel Hill, Stephen J. Fletcher and the staff of the North Carolina Collection Photographic Archives shepherded us through their vast collections. Sherman Hayes, librarian of UNC Wilmington's William Madison Randall Library, and the Cape Fear Museum's Ruth Haas and Tim Bottoms graciously granted us access to the transcripts and photographs in their outstanding exhibit/project "World War II: Through the Eyes of the Cape Fear."

Other people from various organizations and museums also steered us toward remarkable histories and images, including Joe Noah and Sam Sox Jr. of the Preddy Memorial Foundation; the General William C. Lee Airborne Museum in Dunn; the Graveyard of the Atlantic Museum on Hatteras Island; the North Carolina Transportation Museum in Spencer; Jane Johnson, information specialist in the Carolina Room of the Charlotte-Mecklenburg County Public Library; Museum Services Director Kim Sincox at the Battleship *North Carolina* Memorial in Wilmington; Jane Martin, The Photo Editor in Virginia; Greensboro *News & Record* image archivist Marcus Green; Special Collections Librarian Beverly Tetterton with the New Hanover County Public Library; Archivist J. Stephen Catlett at the Greensboro Historical Museum; Dr. John Duvall, director of the Airborne and Special Operations Museum in Fayetteville; Brenda Hughes, writer and producer of the documentary "Thank You, Eddie Hart," and Betty Carter of the Women Veterans Historical Collection at UNC Greensboro's Jackson Library.

We extend a special thanks to Tom Colones of WSPA-TV News in Spartanburg, South Carolina, who provided us with photography and the powerful story of James McRacken.

Other individuals also shared memories and photographs, for which we are most appreciative: Norman and Petie Lynn Bass, Don Bolden, John Bumgarner, Anita Price Davis, Norris and Dorothy Dearmon, Wilson Eagleson, Barbara Gouge, Lee Grant, Bud Hampton, Patty Long Hill, Betty Russell Hurd, H.G. Jones, Nancy Kimmons, James Lancaster, Doc Long, Myrtis McRacken Manus, Hugh Morton, Charles Paty, Michelle Chang-Sherrard, Jo Watts Williams, Ira David Wood III, William H. Wood, Al and Stanley Yelverton.

In addition to these and many others who have made this book a reality, no one deserves more recognition than North Carolina's wartime heroes — soldiers and sailors, laborers and entertainers, husbands and wives, parents and children, men and women, young and old. This is their story, a story that deserves to be told — needs to be told — today and for many years to come. — *Mary Best*

CONTRIBUTORS

MARY BEST
Mary Best, editor and associate publisher of Our State Books, is well known to longtime devotees of *Our State* magazine. As editor in chief from 1996 through 2002, she created an engaging and beautifully photographed series of single-topic special issues.

DIANE SILCOX-JARRETT
Freelance writer Diane Silcox-Jarrett is the author of two books, *One Woman's Dream* and *Heroines of the American Revolution: America's Founding Mothers*. She is also a contributor to *North Carolina Churches: Portraits of Grace* and *Our State* magazine.

DAVID LA VERE
A professor of history at the University of North Carolina at Wilmington, David La Vere is a contributor to the pages of *Our State* magazine, as well as the author of numerous professional and academic journals.

JIMMY TOMLIN
Statesville native Jimmy Tomlin has more than 20 years of journalism experience. Currently, he works as a feature writer and columnist for the *High Point Enterprise*. He also is a contributor to a variety of regional and national publications, including *Our State* magazine. He has received numerous state and national writing awards, including first place in the 2003 Amy Writing Awards, a competition that honors biblical truth in writing.

LARRY WILLIAMS
Having joined the *Our State* magazine staff in 2000 as an ad designer, Larry Williams has become an invaluable member of the Our State team and became the art director of Our State Books in 2003. He graduated from Elon University with a degree in finance and studied and worked abroad before choosing North Carolina as his home.

BIBLIOGRAPHY

PUBLISHED SOURCES

Adams, Michael C.C. *The Best War Ever: America and World War II*. Baltimore: Johns Hopkins University Press, 1994.

Ambrose, Stephen E. *Band of Brothers: E. Company, 506th Regiment, 101st Airborne from Normandy to Hitler's Eagle Nest*. New York: Simon & Schuster, 1992.

——. *Citizen Soldiers: The U.S. Army from the Normandy Beaches to the Bulge to the Surrender of Germany*. New York: Simon & Schuster, 1997.

Bigger, Margaret G. *World War II — Hometown and Home Front Heroes*. Charlotte, N.C.: A. Borough Books, 2003.

Billinger, Robert D. Jr. "Behind the Wire: German Prisoners of War at Camp Sutton, 1944-1946." *North Carolina Historical Review* 61 (October 1994): 481-504.

Blee, Ben W. Capt. *Battleship North Carolina (BB-55)*. Wilmington, N.C.: USS North Carolina Battleship Commission, 1982.

Boyle, David. *World War II: A Photographic History*. New York: Barnes & Noble Books, 1998.

Bradley, James with Ron Powers. *Flags of Our Fathers: Heroes of Iwo Jima*. New York: Bantam Books, 2000.

Brokaw, Tom. *The Greatest Generation*. New York: Random House, 1998.

Bumgarner, John R., M.D. *Parade of the Dead*. Jefferson, N.C.: McFarland & Company Inc., 1995.

Claiborne, Jack. *The Charlotte Observer: Its Time and Place, 1869-1986*. Chapel Hill, N.C.: University of North Carolina Press, 1986.

Colones, Thomas S. "The Savior of Mayenne." Spartanburg, S.C.:WSPA-TV CBS, 2004.

Davis, Anita Price. *Real Heroes*. Spartanburg, S.C.: Honoribus Press, 2002.

Davis, Anita and James M. Walker. *Rutherford County in World War II*, Vol. 1. Charleston, S.C.: Arcadia Publishing, 2003.

Dew, Stephen Herman. *The Queen City at War: Charlotte, North Carolina During World War II 1939-1945*. Lanham, Md.: University Press of America, 2001.

Edwards, Bob. *Edward R. Murrow and the Birth of Broadcast Journalism*. Hoboken, N.J.: John Wiley & Sons Inc., 2004.

Freedom's Heroes: True Stories from Those Who Lived Them. Greensboro, N.C.: Senior Resources of Guilford, 2002.

Goodwin, Doris Kearns. *No Ordinary Time: Franklin and Eleanor Roosevelt: The Home Front in World War II*. New York: Simon and Schuster, 1994.

Hickman, Homer H. Jr. *Torpedo Junction*. Annapolis, Md.: Naval Institute Press, 1989.

Hughes, Brenda. "Thank You, Eddie Hart." 2004.

I'll Be Seeing You: 50 Songs of World War II. Milwaukee, Wis.: Hal Leonard Corporation, 1995.

Jones, H.G. *North Carolina Illustrated, 1524-1984*. Chapel Hill, N.C.: University of North Carolina Press, 1983.

Jones, Wilbur D. Jr. *A Sentimental Journey: Memoirs of a Wartime Boomtown*. Shippensburg, Penn.: White Mane Books, 2002.

Krammer, Arnold. *Nazi Prisoners of War in America*. New York: Stein and Day, 1979.

Lemmon, Sarah McCulloh. *North Carolina's Role in World War II*. Raleigh, N.C.: Division of Archives and History, North Carolina Department of Cultural Resources, 1964.

Life: Our Finest Hour: The Triumphant Spirit of America's World War II Generation. New York: Time Inc., 2000.

Lyons, Michael J. *World War II: A Short History*. Upper Saddle River, N.J.: Prentice Hall, 2004.

Miller, Donald L. *The Story of World War II*. New York: Simon & Schuster, 1945.

Morgan, Robert Col. USAFR, Ret. with Ron Powers. *The Man Who Flew the Memphis Belle: Memoir of a WWII Bomber Pilot*. New York: Penguin Putnam Inc., 2001.

Powell, Lew. *On This Day in North Carolina*. Winston-Salem, N.C.: John F. Blair, Publisher. 1996.

Powell, William S. *North Carolina Through Four Centuries*. Chapel Hill, N.C.: University of North Carolina Press, 1989.

Terkel, Studs. *"The Good War": An Oral History of World War II*. New York: The New Press, 1984.

Van Der Vat, Dan. *Pearl Harbor: The Day of Infamy — An Illustrated History*. New York: Basic Books, 2001.

Willmott, H.P., Robin Cross, and Charles Messenger. *World War II*. London: DK Publishing Inc., 2004.

Wise, Nancy Baker and Christy Wise. *A Mouthful of Rivets: Women at Work in World War II*. San Francisco: Jossey-Bass Publishers, 1994.

ONLINE SOURCES

76th Engineer Battalion, U.S. Army, www.atourofduty.homestead.com/76thEngBN8thArmy.html

588th Engineer Battalion, History, U.S. Army, www.hood.army.mil/4id_588th-eng/page3.html

Camp Lejeune, History, U.S. Marine Corps, www.lejeune.usmc.mil/mcb/history.asp

The Home Front, Charlotte–Mecklenburg 1941-1946. Public Library of Charlotte & Mecklenburg County, www.cmstory.org/homefront/main.htm

Cherry Point, History, U.S. Marine Corps, www.cherrypoint.usmc.mil/history.asp

Fort Bragg, History, U.S. Army, www.bragg.army.mil/history/HistoryPage/History%20of%20Fort%20Bragg/fort1.htm

The Men of Montford Point: The First Black Marines, www.geocities.com/nubiansong/montford.htm

Preddy Memorial Foundation, www.preddy-foundation.org/

Tuskegee Airmen, www.fatherryan.org/black-military/tusk.htm

The War Dogs Platoons: Marine Dogs of World War II, www.worldwar2history.info/Marines/dogs.html

COLLECTIONS

The Airborne & Special Operations Museum. Fayetteville, N.C. www.asomf.org/

Greensboro Historical Museum. Greensboro, N.C. www.greensborohistory.org

The North Carolina Collection, Photographic Archives, University of North Carolina at Chapel Hill. Chapel Hill, N.C. www.lib.unc.edu/ncc/photos.html

North Carolina Museum of History. Raleigh, N.C. ncmuseumofhistory.org/

North Carolina Office of Archives and History. Raleigh, N.C. www.ah.dcr.state.nc.us/

Women Veterans Historical Collection, University of North Carolina at Greensboro. Greensboro, N.C. library.uncg.edu/depts/archives/veterans/index.html

"World War II: Through the Eyes of the Cape Fear Exhibit, 1939-2002." William M. Randall Library at the University of North Carolina at Wilmington and the Cape Fear Museum, Wilmington, N.C. capefearww2.uncwil.edu/

INDEX OF NAMES

Gracie Allen, 132
James Bailey, 32
Josiah W. Bailey, 30, 32
Petie Lynn Bass, cover, 172-173
Romare Bearden, 159
Frances Simpson Best, cover, 8-11, 53
Will Best, 8-11, 47
Westray Battle Boyce, 96-97
Omar Bradley, 37
Alice Broughton, 123
J. Melville Broughton, 50, 118, 123, 125, 127
John Bumgarner, cover, 83
George Burns, 132
John Burns, 78
George H.W. Bush, 46
Dan Cameron, 137
Charles Cannon, 159
W.J. Cash, 135
Martin Chaves, 142
Gregg Cherry, 147
Winston Churchill, 27, 60, 71, 150
Lydia Clarke, 49
Mary Clifford, cover, 91
James S. Craig Jr., 160
R. Stafford Cripps, 94
Carol Dare, 127
Anita Price Davis, 21, 115
Charles De Gaulle, 116
Dorothy Dearmon, cover, 138
Norris Dearmon, cover, 138
Karl Dönitz, 57
Norwood Dorman, 75
Tommy Dorsey, 135
J.S. Dorton, 53
Hugh A. Drum, 37
Wilson Eagleson, 66-67
Dwight D. Eisenhower, 37
Ray E. Eubanks, 103
Bill Ferebee, 154
Thomas Ferebee, cover, 154
William Few, 131
Keith Finch, 70
Gerald Ford, 46
Harold J. Fox, 41
Leonard T. Gerow, 37

Barbara Gouge, 95
Betty Grable, 130
Calveen Sherrill Grant, 139
Roy Jack Grant, 139
Dwight Green, 21
Edgar Green, 21
Johan Habets, 169
William David Halyburton Jr., 103
Everett "Bud" Hampton, cover, 86-87
H.S. Hansell, 65
Marion Hargrove, 135
Shuler Eugene Harman, 37
Walter Harrelson, 155
Eddie Hart, cover, 168-169
Hattie Hart, 169
Betty Heath, 166-167
James Edwin "Ed" Heath, 166-167
Rufus G. Herring, 103
Charlton Heston, 49
William S. Hinton, 32
Emperor Hirohito, 147
Adolf Hitler, 148
Courtney H. Hodges, 37
Jack Hoffler, 68
J.R. Holden, cover, 74
Dorothy Hoover, 92
Bob Hope, 132, 140
Brenda Hughes, 169
Betty Russell Hurd, 114
Ese Baxley-Jarrett, 132
Chandler W. Johnson, 89
H.G. Jones, cover, 72-73
John Kimmons, 28-29
Nancy Kimmons, 28-29
James Lancaster, 18-19
Wade Lawrence, 167
William C. Lee, cover, 70-71
Sarah McCulloh Lemmon, 23, 130
Charles Lindbergh, 92, 131
William Henry "Doc" Long, cover, 100-101, 174-175
Joe Louis, 130
Jacklyn Harold Lucas, cover, 102-103
Pete Lynn, 172-173
Ruth Lynn, 172-173

Henry Jay MacMillan, 136-137
Mae McRacken Manus, 116-117
George C. Marshall, 37
Fletcher Martin, 107
Aaron May, 152
J. Lesley McNair, 37
Linda McIntyre, 37
Neil "Hector" McNeill, 89
James Dougald McRacken, 116-117
Myrtis McRacken, 116-117
Martha Pegram Mitchell, 106-107
Dorothy Morgan, 65
Robert K. Morgan, 65-66
Dewey Morrow, 134
Hugh Morton, 140, 160
Edward R. Murrow, 134, 152
Benito Mussolini, 62
Thurman Nail, 128
Mary Nelson, 95
Mary Webb Nicholson, 94
Joe Noah, 110
Richard E. Nugent, 37
George S. Patton Jr., 37
Charles Paty, 79
Nellie Miles Paul, 108
John Payne, 126
Margaret Polk, 65
Lew Powell, 123
Bill Preddy, 110-111
George Preddy, 110-113
Arthur Price, cover, 115
Falls Price, cover, 115
William C. Price Sr. and Jr., 71
Ernie Pyle, 106, 127
Bob Rankin, 151
Virginia Reavis, 105
Buddy Rich, 135
George Rogers, 157
Mickey Rooney, 130
Eleanor Roosevelt, 95, 150, 151
Franklin D. Roosevelt, 8, 11, 14, 16, 17, 44, 55, 150, 151
Kenneth Royall, 162
Richard Rushton, 59

Frank Russell, 114
Harold Russell, 104
Phil Russell, 114
Terry Sanford, 160
John W. Scism, 26
Celeste Shue, 138
James Shue, 138
William H. Simpson, 37
Frank Sinatra, 135
Kate Smith, 132
Walter Bedell Smith, 37
Carl Spaatz, 37
Jo Stafford, 135
James R. Starns, 6-7
Ralph F. Stearley, 37
Jeff Thigpen, 49
Archie Thomas, 114
John G. Thomas, 122
Patty Thomas, 140
Max Thompson, 103
Viola Thompson, cover, 91
Paul Tibbetts, 154
Harry S. Truman, 76, 150
LuAnne Tywater, 167
Gordon Vaeth, 56
Hoyt S. Vanderberg, 37
Millie Veasey, 93
Betty Habets-Vrancken, 169
Wallace Wade, 142
Raymond Wagoner, cover, 74
James M. Walker, 21
Henry F. Warner, 103
Blanchard Watts, cover
Otto P. Weyland, 37
Gordon Whittiker, 85
L.M. Wilkerson, 146
Alice Wahab William, 57
Ted Williams, 141
Walter Winchell, 118
Ethel Wise, 159
Carroll Wood, 170-171
Ira David Wood III, 170-171
William H. Wood, cover, 84
Jane Wyman, 126
Isoroku Yamamoto, 16, 85
Al Yelverton, 139
Stanley Yelverton, 139

ABOUT OUR STATE BOOKS

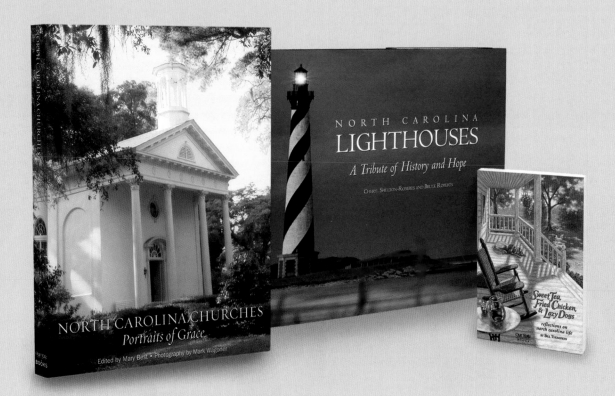

Founded in 2003, Our State Books celebrates North Carolina's lively culture, natural beauty, and rich heritage by publishing books that exemplify the Tar Heel experience. Our readers — loyal, astute, and with a keen eye for detail and superior writing — expect works of unparalleled quality on subjects of interest to those who live in, visit, or simply cherish the Old North State.

Our State Books is a division of Mann Media, publisher of *Our State* magazine. Continually published since 1933, *Our State* is North Carolina's only monthly travel, history, and folklore publication and is enjoyed by more than half a million readers each month. Our State Books evolved from our readers' desire to learn more about their adored home state in a photographically intensive, friendly, and intelligent manner.

On average, Our State Books releases three to four original books a year and employs many of the same writers and photographers who have made *Our State* magazine one of the most successful regional magazines in the nation. Subject areas include North Carolina general-interest nonfiction, travel, culture, history, religion, gardening, nature, art and architecture, essays and memoirs, food, and photography.

Recent titles include *North Carolina Churches: Portraits of Grace*, edited by Mary Best and photographed by Mark Wagoner; *North Carolina Lighthouses: A Tribute of History and Hope* by Cheryl Shelton-Roberts and Bruce Roberts and *Sweet Tea, Fried Chicken, and Lazy Dogs: Reflections on North Carolina Life* by Bill Thompson.

A NATION REMEMBERS
Made of Mount Airy granite, 56 pillars representing every state and territory in the union in the early 1940s symbolize American unity at the World War II Memorial in Washington, D.C.

NORTH CAROLINA